Stories of Rell Sunn: Queen of Mākaha

~

Compiled by Greg Ambrose

Edited by Karyl Reynolds

Bess Press, Inc. 〉 3565 Harding Avenue 〉 Honolulu 〉 Hawaiʻi 〉 www.BessPress.com

Book and cover design by Mariko Merritt.

Cataloging-in-publication data

Ambrose, Greg.
  Stories of Rell Sunn : queen of
Makaha / Greg Ambrose.
        p.   cm.
  Includes illustrations.
  ISBN-13: 978-157306-3234
  ISBN-10: 157306-3231
  1. Sun, Rell, 1950-1998. 2. Surfers -
Hawaii. 3 Women surfers - Hawaii.
  I. Title.
  GV838.S86 2010   797.3-dc22

Printed and bound in China through Colorcraft Ltd., Hong Kong

CONTENTS

AMBASSADOR OF STRENGTH & SPIRIT

"Rell Rides the Skies" painted by Dan Fletcher

Introduction

IF YOU DIDN'T know Rell Sunn, now is your chance to discover a remarkable woman. You would have liked Rell at first meeting, as she had the gift of making anyone feel like he or she was the most special person in the world. With her cheerful "*aloha*," a hug, and a kiss, you felt like you had just made a friend for life.

And what a friend. This strong, slender, Chinese-Hawaiian-Irish woman from Hawai'i's rugged Wai'anae Coast on the island of O'ahu was a renaissance woman of sorts—a founder and top competitor on the women's world professional surfing tour, a free-diving spearfisher who could dive deeper and bring back more fish than most men, O'ahu's first female lifeguard, radio disc jockey, single mom, teacher, artist, hula dancer, outrigger canoe paddler, TV sports commentator, mentor and role model to youngsters, fierce protector of the oppressed, and worldwide ambassador of *aloha*.

The first time I saw Rell Sunn, I was just a kid, growing up in Kailua on the windward side of O'ahu. As a young surfer during the early '60s, I had never seen any girls surfing. Then, one day, my dad told my siblings and me that he was taking us to a surf contest way on the other side of the island in Mākaha.

There, in front of me, I found many of my surf heroes, local and from around the world. To my astonishment, among the contestants, were three mermaids—Rell and her sisters Val and Kula. Not only were these girls beautiful, but they were also tearing up the waves with style and grace. And I was beguiled.

Years passed, and I got a job at the *Honolulu Star-Bulletin* as the ocean reporter—a dream assignment that allowed me to write everything about the ocean and the island that I loved. Some of the most satisfying stories I wrote featured Rell and her many adventures as an all-around waterwoman. More importantly, through, with our shared love of the ocean, she became my friend.

Many a morning, out in Wai'anae working on a story for the newspaper, I'd spot perfect waves but, sadly, I'd have no board with me. I only had to knock on Rell's door. She'd point to the numerous surfboards stacked into the rafters of her carport, and, with a twinkle in her eye, say, "Take your pick." Many times she'd go out with me.

I never knew a person as generous and talented and full of life as Rell. Now, with this book, you'll get to know a little about her, too.

The format of my book is simple but powerful. Rell's friends tell, in their own words, what Rell Sunn meant to them and how their lives were changed by knowing her. This book is written in the traditional "talk-story" style of Hawai'i, which maintains the flavor of these remarkable stories as they are told by Rell's friends. Enjoy.

Forever Young ⟩ Greg Ambrose

STANDING ON A boulder at Chun's Reef on a splendid Hawaiian winter morning, it appeared that every one of the peeling head-high to overhead waves was embraced by more than one ardent suitor. *Bummahs*. And, yet, as I watched the feeding frenzy, I realized that a few of the takeoff spots were unguarded.

Leaving my wife and her girlfriend on the beach to talk story, I stroked my shortboard into the mix of longboarders, shortboarders, and bodyboarders, balancing the disappointment of waves snatched by others in a better position with the triumph of snagging some choice screamers from the pack.

Finally, pleased with my success, I rode a wave nearly to the beach just in time to tear into the picnic lunch the girls had prepared. Life was good.

And, then, while savoring the *kaukau* and plotting my strategy for the next session, an anomaly piqued my curiosity. Some local girl on a longboard, who I judged to be a teen-ager due to her lithe shape and seemingly endless energy, was putting on a clinic with her wave riding. Her timing was impeccable; her moves a splendid blend of grace and aggression. She was catching the deepest set waves and dancing her way to the channel. The more I watched, the more intrigued I became, as her recklessness said "youth" while her style said "experience."

I thought I knew all of the local longboard *wahine* on the North Shore, but this one was a mystery. When the anomaly continued to torment me, I paddled out for a closer look. I cut across the lineup just in time to see the mystery wahine blazing down the line at top speed, effortlessly pumping her board for more speed, her long hair flying and a wicked grin on her face as she sprayed me with a cutback. Mystery solved.

"Rell, you look like a teenager. Your hair is back. You're surfing like a maniac," I said as we both paddled out to the lineup.

"I feel like I could live forever," she said. "The last treatment was really rough, but now I feel great. I have energy, strength, and no more *bolohead*," she said, laughing, her eyes twinkling with mischief as she whipped her hair from side to side.

An already good session became pure magic as we raced each other for waves and splashed each other with cutbacks or bottom turns whenever possible. But, the best part was talking about how each of us and our loved ones were doing and expressing confidence that the worst was behind Rell.

Whenever I think of Rell, the image that comes to mind is of that day. Rell…full of life and at the peak of her surfing performance…a true *keiki o ke kai*.

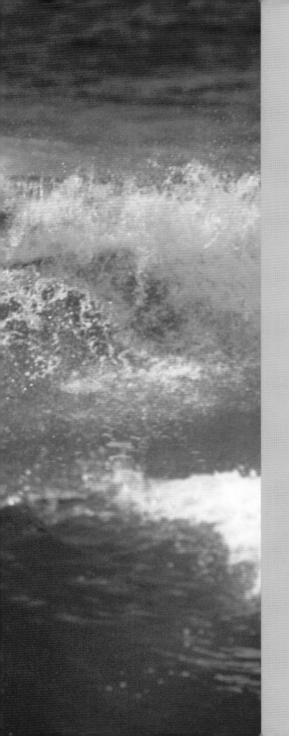

The World's
Waterwoman

Perpetually in Motion 〉 Greg Ambrose

(Written in 1982 for the Honolulu Star-Bulletin)

THEY SHOULD HAVE listened to Buffalo.

Back in '60, the City and County engineers decided that the bathhouse at Mākaha Beach Park should go *makai* of Farrington Highway, and Buffalo Keaulana shook his head.

Drawing upon a lifetime of experience in the ocean, in general, and at Mākaha, in particular, Buffalo warned the engineers that the waves would wash the bathhouse right into the ocean. Although the giant waves of December '69 left the bathhouse standing, a huge swell in the winter of '82 fulfilled Buffalo's grim prophecy.

These days, the Mākaha regulars who used the bathhouse as their clubhouse hold court under an old *hau* tree. Residing over the court sessions is Rell Sunn, one of the loveliest water women of the Leeward Coast. Old timers, such as the ageless Buffalo and Homer Barrett, and members of the younger generation kick back to play tandem *'ukulele* and sing the old songs. It seems that time has passed the beach at Mākaha entirely. From nearby Tower 47-A, City and County lifeguard Sunn keeps a watchful eye on her beach. Laughing and joking with the boys one minute, solicitous of an elderly tourist couple walking by the next, Sunn belongs at Mākaha Beach.

"My dad always teases me. He says, 'I passed by and saw you smiling and talking. That's not working.'"

Whether she's greeting old friends or making new ones, Sunn moves with a natural grace that characterizes all her actions. She has friends everywhere, and, when she directs her radiant smile at you, you feel certain you have made a friend for life.

Sunn carries her thirty-two years lightly, and she has spent nearly all of them at Mākaha. She started surfing at the age of four, and she takes to the ocean with the ease and frequency of a mermaid. Similarly, she has a mermaid's need for frequent and prolonged immersion in saltwater to insure her physical and emotional well-being. Adept at spearfishing and a champion surfer, she turns to the ocean for food, for exercise, for fun, and especially for solace.

The ocean isn't her whole life; it's just the best part of it. "It seems like beach people are happier than other people," she says.

Sunn also finds an outlet for her artistic ability by dancing with the *Pi'o Mai Na Lehua halau*. Plus, she's a published writer possessing a sensitive insight and who can pluck words out of the air and string them into sentences lovelier than any *lei*. Her other credits include stints in front of the cameras for numerous surf movies, TV shows, and commercials.

With so many demands on her time, this Kamehameha Schools graduate manages to steal precious hours to develop and run surf contests for kids on the Leeward side and to coordinate the surf trials for professional women hopefuls during the winter competitions. However, her main claim to fame is her prowess as a professional surfer. Sunn started competing at the age of fourteen, but, back then, she was too shy to compete aggressively. "I remember when my sister and I used to compete. We couldn't sleep at night because we were upset we might have to beat each other in the contest," she says.

With countless contests behind her, Sunn has left any shyness behind while retaining compassion for her fellow competitors. She feels right at home going stroke for stroke with the men in Buffalo's annual longboard classic, but her greatest success has come on shortboards against other women. "I'm more of an everyday surfer, although I enjoy the contests because I like to see what the pros are up to and to promote surfing to help it survive."

Sunn was devastated recently when tests revealed a malignant breast tumor. Surgery and radiation treatment appear to have ended the problem, and a sore and weakened Sunn is busy getting back in shape for this winter's professional surfing competition on the North Shore.

The crew that surfs Mākaha includes some of the roughest surfers on O'ahu. But, Sunn paints an almost idyllic picture of life on the Leeward side. "The guys out here aren't so insecure that they hold you back. That's one of the good things about life in the country—they help you out, and there's no ego trip. We ladies have it made."

Sunn is a contract worker with the City and County, which gives her the flexibility she needs to compete on the professional surfing circuit. She went to the mainland this summer to surf in contests in Atlantic City and California, where she placed third and fourth, respectively. "Not bad for the oldest contestant there." This winter, Sunn will be busy running the women's trials for the Sunkist World Cup at Hale'iwa, as well as surfing after some of the $15,000 prize money herself. In the spring, she plans to follow the contest trail "down under" to Australia, where a trio of contests for women makes it the most lucrative stop on the circuit.

Life on the road competing may have its attractions, but Sunn is always drawn back to her beach at Mākaha. "I've been almost everyplace else, and I love it here. I'll always come back."

It's a close-knit group that surfs and plays at Mākaha, although there are others who think of the beach as theirs, even though they haven't spent much of their lives there. "We have the newly wed, the nearly dead, and the down the lines…the beach crowd from the Makaha Towers…to liven things up," Sunn says. But, it's the regulars who make for the most interesting stories. Like the time Teddy Bear spotted a deer swimming in the waves at Mākaha…"We don't know how it got there, but Teddy Bear speared it and we *huli-hulied* it on the beach."

"You don't believe it, but we pay the newspapers to print stories about crime on the Wai'anae Coast. It keeps people from moving here," she says with a sly smile.

Although she is the master of a dangerous sport, after twenty-nine years of surfing, her worst incident occurred only five years ago. Sunn was paddling into a wave at Mākaha when a longboarder ran in to her. The collision split one of her kidneys and left a sexy scar snaking down from her sternum to her hip. Still, incidents like that haven't slowed her reckless assault on the waves.

"I'll gracefully bow out when I can't cut it anymore. I'm double [hot, young, Aussie surfer] Pam Burridge's age. But, when you come from Mākaha, there's no such thing as time…as aging. We're all just old kids."

Wisdom From the Master 〉 Rabbit Kekai

WHEN THEY WERE small and we used to sit on the beach, Kula would come down, and Rell used to tag along with her big sister. Sometimes, I would tell Kula a thing, and Rell would say, "How do you do that?" So, I would explain everything to her just like Duke taught me.

"When you dance hula, you gotta think. When you surf, you gotta think. Every wave is different. It's not the same wave that you can do the same thing on. It changes. Sometimes it breaks a little farther in, sometimes a little farther out. Then, you come by the shallows and it's coming over, falling over fast. You gotta look at that and adjust."

"When you get outside, you can do that 'Rell Sunn' kind of maneuver, real nice and smooth and everything."

"That's you, Rell," I always used to tell her. And she still had that, down to the end.

She started to get real good. One day, we had a big swell out here at Mākaha, and I caught her out of the corner of my eye. So, I wen' lift my board up, and, zoom, she went right on past me. Then, just like a floater, I came down. I was following her, and she did a roundhouse cutback right at me. So, I lifted my board up again.

She came to me and said, "I didn't see you behind, and thought you wen' kick out."

And I said, "Good. You know what you learned? The cutback and how to get out of there fast. Long time I told you that. Now, you got to do that all the time."

Little things like that I taught her, the finer points. She got good. After that, we were inseparable.

A Delicate Touch ⟩ Rabbit Kekai

WHEN SHE FIRST started to try noseriding, Rell used to fall and couldn't run back (to the center of the board). I told her, "Rell, you ever see a road with glass over there and there is no place for you to walk except for on the glass? How you going walk? You going walk real light, eh? Same thing on the board—you just got to make your feet light when you go up like that. Keep your body like it's suspended, but your feet move light. Then, when you walk back, same thing, keep your feet light."

She said, "What you call that?"

And I said, "Pussyfoot, just like how the cat walks. Pussyfoot. You cannot hear a cat walk."

She got to be so good on the nose, do that "cheater five," one of the best I've seen out here. She looked so damn good.

When they honored her down at Oceanside at the museum there, I had to make a speech. If I didn't have dark glasses, boy, I wouldn't have been able to talk. Tears was just rolling down. Everybody in there couldn't believe what I said about her, and Rell was crying, too. She came up and just hugged me, and I gave her the microphone, and she couldn't say anything.

The Call of the Ocean ⟩ Kathy Terada

WE WERE PRACTICING for a hula competition, and the chant we were doing was about the place names all around the coast.

So, what we did that day was go to every site and dance. And, when we got to Mākaha, Rell just had to go out and surf during a break. And she caught about a zillion waves. She was the only one who went out. The rest of us just watched her. I remember watching her 'cause she would just paddle out, catch a wave, paddle out, catch a wave.

We were chanting and dancing in the sand at each place…all the way down from Ka'ena Point. But, the chant was about the beach, too.

The call of the ocean is strong. That's how come we left hula. We took hula one night a week, and, on Saturday was the *kahiko* class. [*Kahiko* involved] training to become a dance instructor and chanter, and we had to chant to come into class. We'd come straight from the surf, all wet. Sometimes we weren't allowed into class until we were mentally ready and chanted and, then, got in.

I remember, at one point, the *kumu* asked us, "What's more important—surfing or hula?"

And we said, "I guess surfing."

The Woman Who Shot Ulua Valence 〉 Rell Sunn

'A'ohe ia e loa'a aku, he ulua kāpapa no ka moana.
"He cannot be caught for he is an *ulua* fish of the deep ocean."
(said in admiration of a warrior who will not give up without a struggle)

REACTION TIME IS faster when you see bigger fish. At the instant I saw the forty-five pound *ulua* munching on a tiny snowflake eel, my Hawaiian sling hand spear was already cranked and flying. The three prongs lodged in the back of his blunt head, and he spun once, eyeing me with reproach. But, instead of screeching for the channel, he turned and went back to work on the eel. I was faster and luckier with my backup spear, as it found its mark between his eyes. The *ulua* bolted for the deep blue of the drop-off, the two spears poking like antennae from his brow, and humming through the water with his furious rush.

It had been an easy, almost effortless dive day. The usually temperamental waters off of O'ahu's Ka'ena Point were placid, seemingly beaten into laziness by the summer heat. The ocean here is full of fish, outrageous holes, and Hawaiian myth and lore. I had paddled out on my long-board, which was both my partner and diving platform, with two Hawaiian sling spears, a mask, a snorkel, fins, and a dive bag, all weighing no more than fifteen pounds, board included. Within an hour, the nine-foot, six-inch longboard was awash under the weight of sixty-five pounds of octopus, giant *uhu* (parrotfish), and a couple of seven-pound *kūmū* (highly prized goatfish—red, good, delicious). I was already headed in and skipping over a mental shopping list for the ingredients needed for steaming the *kūmū* and stuffing and baking the *uhu* when I spotted my dream fish.

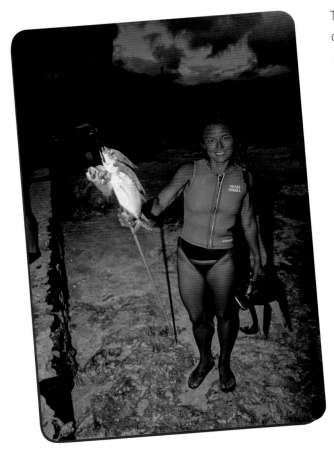

The *ulua* had put some distance between us, despite the two spears stuck into him. I was already three-quarters of a mile out and swimming against the current with burning lungs and muscles. My board had drifted down current. It was a gamble to let it go and swim after the fish, but I couldn't afford to lose sight of my quarry for even a second. I was committed to the gamble.

The wobbling of the spears soon wore the *ulua* down enough so that I could use the rest of my energy to surge ahead of him and herd him back toward the shallows. As my calves began to cramp, I was relieved to see the fish doing flips and violent spirals. He was dying.

Ulua are beautiful fish. They're smart, good hunters, and incredibly strong. I've seen them turn vicious when injured. As this *ulua* fluttered to a ledge thirty-five feet below, I realized that he didn't know that particular crevice as well as I did. It was a dead end. It was the stroke of luck I needed to take a chance on retrieving my board. Three minutes later, I was back with my board, hovering over the crevice, and relaxing my breathing to get a good gulp of air for the descent.

The *ulua* was scraping the spears against the ceiling of the ledge when I reached the opening. I sunk the fingers of one hand into his eye socket, gripped the spear shaft protruding from his head with the other, and began to guide him out and up toward the surface. He fought the hardest two feet from the surface. My legs were still cramping, and I was on the verge of blacking out. Then, I shot out into the air, blasting the snorkel free of water and, for the first time, felt the true heft of the fish like a leaden umbrella held overhead.

As I wrestled the *ulua* up onto the deck of my board, I heard what sounded like wind blowing rough reel lines or dogs barking. I pulled my mask off and followed the noise to a spot on the shoreline where four fishermen were jumping, yelling, and pointing at me. I grinned and raised the forty-five-pound trophy in a victory salute. Then, I turned my head back seaward just in time to see a fourteen-foot tiger shark sliding under the surface barely fifty feet away, knifing toward my board, my sixty-five pounds of octopus, my other fish, my *ulua*, and my legs, not necessarily in that order.

A million heartbreaking thoughts and possibilities flashed into my mind, yet I had but two solutions to them all. Pulling myself into a less-exposed, knee-paddling position I scuttled the *ulua* off the side of my board, took a few pulls toward shore and said aloud, "I'll be back. Next time, catch your own dinner!" I didn't have the heart to do the "panic-paddle" in, and, so, from a safe distance, I watched my dream fish start to sink. He wasn't even a foot under when the tiger shark grabbed him and tore into the midsection. My lungs, my arms, and the fishermen were screaming as I paddled away from the snapping, churning, orgy.

From shore, the fishermen and I watched the shark finish up what could have been a mini-*luau* for my neighbors and me. We traded fish recipes, shark stories, and other spooky stuff about Ka'ena. They helped clean (and eat) the remaining fish. Other than that fourteen-foot tiger shark, my day could not have been nicer, sharing the day's catch and making new friends.

These men helped me lift my V.W. bug and turn it toward Mākaha. (It had no reverse gear.) And I headed off to my hula class, late again.

I drove along the dirt road back to Mākaha, the sparkling afternoon sea smoldering against the rock-bound shore. In less than a half-hour, I would be back in my more landlocked world, full of Hawaiian music, dancing, and talking story with the girls. But, out there, under the deceptively placid surface, was a world blind to gender. Though I was taught by men, I was formed by and subjected to the rigid laws of a seemingly lawless realm that treated me and every grazing *ulua* or marauding shark with the same utter equanimity.

Though I was running late, I stopped along the way and picked some *hinahina* for my hula sisters' *lei*. The succulent flowers grow along the arid Ka'ena coast road, living on the thick sea spray. Not exactly *ulua* steaks, but Pua and Sweets and the girls would be stoked.

A similar version of this tale can be read on Rell's website at rellsunn.com.

A Fish Tale 〉 Rell Sunn via Mark Cunningham

I LIKE TO GO diving off my surfboard. I like to catch *kūmū*, *menpachi*, *a'weoweo*, and *uhu*. Good fun. You know how legends are made? I'll tell you a story.

I was out before work one morning when I was guarding at Nānākuli. I was diving way outside at this hole in about forty feet, and, just beyond that, it's deeper. I saw Buff coming my way, and it surprised me.

He's paddling his board, and I said, "Hey! What are you doing way out here?"

He says, "I don't know, but somebody better start the fire," because we both had fish already.

I said, "You came by yourself?"

"Yeah, I came from Ulehawa. We were talkin' sharks, and these two *panties* left me. They're still in the truck talking about the sharks."

Jimmy and Kana Boy didn't go out, so Buff was out there by himself.

I'm catching octopus when Buff spears this huge *ulua* with his arbalete, and it goes down in a cave. I never use an arbalete. I should, but they're too easy. I love three-prongs. I like a little sport.

So, Buff swims up to me and goes, "Rell, my fish wen' in da' cave, and you gotta go get it because da sharks gonna come and get it if one of us don't go get it."

I say, "You go get it."

"No. Uh-uh. I can't. You go get it. Hurry up befo' da' sharks go get 'em."

We're always playing practical jokes on one another. So, I didn't trust him. I know it's a set-up.
"Buff, is the shark in that cave already?"

"Hurry up. You gotta go now or there will be."

So, I go down with my little three-prong just in case.
I want to hit this fish with my little three-prong,
and I hear, "Tink, tink, tink."

George Downing and
Buffalo Keaulana: two top
bulls of the beach conduct
affairs in Mākaha.

That big *ulua* and the arbalete are just bouncing off the sides of the cave, dang it. So, I go up for more air and coaching. It's only forty to forty-five feet deep, maybe deeper, and I go back down, and Buff's pointing to the other side. So, I swim over there, go under the ledge, and pull the fish out.

It is huge. I'm trying to come up with it, and it's fighting me. It's like an umbrella, so I can barely pull it up. I can't point him up 'cause he's fighting so hard. I thought I was gonna drown. So, five feet from the surface, Buff decides to come down and help. Oh, I was so mad at him.

We go in to the beach, and he cuts the fish right in half. He gives me the tail half, and he takes the head part. "Here's your half," he says. And, then, because he was out of shape at that time and he couldn't tell the guys that he couldn't dive forty-five feet, he told everybody, "You know, Rell? She can dive eighty to a hundred feet easy." I just kinda kept quiet because that's how legends are made.

A Dream Wave at Last ⟩ Bruce Jenkins

IN MORE THAN forty years of romance with the ocean, I had never caught a wave in my dreams. On the beaches of the subconscious, something always went wrong. No board. No wax. No way down the cliff. I watched gorgeous, pristine waves being ridden by everyone else, but not for me. In my dreams, I never set foot in the ocean.

Then, one day, I lived a dream. I had just become acquainted with Rell Sunn, and I was out bodysurfing a four foot to six foot day at her cherished Mākaha. It was an unforgettable experience just to be out there, diving into the clear blue water, face inches from the reef,

as the likes of Buffalo Keaulana, Mel Pu'u, Dave Parmenter, Rell, and a dozen wonderful women surfers glided above me. Then, a wave came my way. It was vintage Mākaha. You couldn't *not* make it. Trimming along in a high-line flow, arms tucked back, I had time to survey the beach, the lifeguard tower, the formidable mountain range as a tapering shoulder unfolded in front of me… heaven on earth. Then, Rell Sunn appeared, paddling earnestly toward the lineup with a smile. "Yeah!" she cried out. "Whoo!"

Mel Pu'u has spent a lifetime keeping people safe as Mākaha Beach lifeguard.

I never claimed to be a close friend or confidant of Rell's. But, like so many thousands of people, I was touched by her, made by her to feel special for just a moment.

A Perfect Season
Burl Burlingame

WHEN I WENT to college starting in 1971, I became the editor of the Leeward Community College newspaper *Kui Ka Lono*, which means "spreading the news." My sports editor was Rell Sunn. It was a typical student newspaper, and we were goofing around a lot.

Rell wasn't a famous surfer then. But, we knew she liked to surf and that she was good at it. So, we were talking one day and we said, "Why aren't there surf teams?" I think we had read something about one of the California schools having a surf team, like a sports team. "So, we're going to create a surf team—the Leeward Community College surf team. Rell will surf, and I'll be the coach, and we'll challenge all the other schools to meets." Basically, the other schools would not be able to field a team, so we would win by default. That way, the Leeward Community College surf team became the statewide champs.

We determined that my contribution to coaching would be to say to Rell, before she went surfing, "Get out there, and surf like hell. I'll stay here and have a beer."

And she'd go, "Okay, coach."

She'd run out and surf for awhile and come back, and I'd say, "Any other teams show up?"

And she'd say, "No."

And I'd say, "Okay, we won by default." Most of the contests were in the Barbers Point area, at White Plains beach.

She was undefeated. The Leeward Community College surf team was undefeated in its first and only season.

That's my claim to fame…I was Rell Sunn's first surf coach. For years, Rell tried to get me to pierce my ear…to wear an earring because she thought I was a radical. I pierced my ear the day she died.

Riding the Magic Bus 〉 Dan "Skydog" Highland

I LIKE THE one where, the whole time, we were staying with Rell. I was saying, "I want to go surf the North Shore. I have to surf the North Shore."

So, Rell said, "Dan, just get up early tomorrow morning and take the van. You go."

Someone had loaned her a giant Ford van—bright yellow with big purple and blue and orange balls painted on it. On the side, it said "Kama'aina Child Care." So, I threw the boards in the back and set out early in the morning before anyone was on the road. The only people

I saw were bus drivers, and every one of them was waving at me. So, I'd wave back. Finally, I realized that we all looked the same driving those buses.

I pulled up at Sunset Beach and talked to Mike Diffenderfer and a friend of his while we were all checking out the waves. For days, the Triple Crown had been canceled because the waves were too small. But, it was my kind of surf—head high and double overhead toward the point a little bit. I looked at it, and it looked pretty good. So, I said, "I'm going out. The tide's going to change, and it's going get crowded pretty soon because it's going to get good."

The only other person out was Felipe Pomar. Pretty soon, Caroline Zimmerman and Sam paddled out and about a half a dozen Brazilian boogieboard women. They were the friendliest girls around, talking perfect English. Then, they got by themselves, and you couldn't understand a word they were saying.

We surfed for three hours. I got stuck in traffic on the way home, but the bus drivers were still waving at me.

A Wet and Wild New Year 〉 Sonja Evensen

THE OTHER THING that Rell corralled me into was that first night we went surfing at midnight to celebrate the new year. It's the best way to do it because you don't need to get drunk.

We'd meet at Mākaha. The first year, there were only a few of us…she and Brian and me…only three or four of us who went out. I said, "Are you crazy? Okay, though, I'll do it."

"At quarter to twelve, paddle out and catch the first wave of the new year." That was her idea.

And I'm like, "Okay. So, it's midnight and cold, and you're drinking coffee and trying to wake up and putting your wet suit on and turning on your car's headlights to see what you're doing." That first year wasn't so bad, but, the second year, the waves were huge. You could see the whitewater from the beach. A couple years later, she had a following. There was a canoe, and everybody was there. It turned into a favorite thing.

One time, we had glow sticks around our necks so we could see each other. That was a good idea. I remember being the last one out 'cause everybody else caught a wave. I go, "I better hurry up and catch one." Then, fish started jumping, and I went, "Eewwww."

That year, there were a lot of people. There were all these cars, and they turned on their head-lights. If you had a full moon, no problem. But, that year, there wasn't a full moon. There was a canoe out there, though. How crazy is that?!

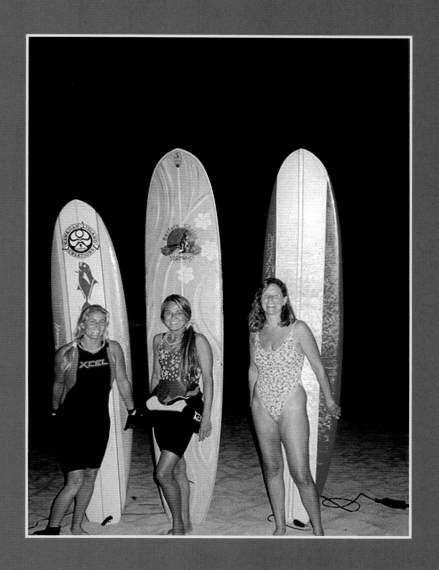

Rell Would Make You Go 〈 Marilyn Link

THERE'S "EDDIE WOULD GO," and Rell would *make you* go. Sometimes, when I'm afraid to do something, I tell myself, "Rell would make me do it."

I'm not a water person. I mean, I am and I'm not. I don't like to go too far from shore. I like the immediacy of knowing, in a couple of strokes, that I can be back on land. If you went out diving with Rell, you'd be on the surfboard, and her famous last words were, "Oh, this is just going to be a quick one."

Three hours later, you're still out there. I remember one time telling her, "Don't make me have to come get you," like I could.

She scared me sometimes because she was getting sick, and I knew she didn't have the breath. I'd be on the board laying the surface, trembling, and I'd look down, 'cause I always had a mask. I'd watch her go down, and I'd try to hold my breath while she was down. I'm starting to gasp, and, then, she disappears in a hole. That's when I'm thinking to myself, "Don't make me come get you." Of course, if I waited long enough, she'd materialize with a fish on her spear. I couldn't let her know that I was freaked out, so I'd be like, "Wow! How nice. Okay, can we go now?"

I think she knew I was a detriment to her out there. But, why would she encourage me to come with her if she knew how I was? I think she would encourage it because she knew there was something for me to gain by it. I mean, I probably walked away a little taller every time, after I calmed myself down. I was better for it.

Then, one time, we went out with Homer [Barrett] without boards, only boogie boards, and went way out at Mākaha. Rell took off, and I was back with Homer.

Homer was sick then, too. And he kind of talked me through it because I'm going, "Whaah, I think I'm ready to go back."

And he goes, "Naaah, pretty soon, pretty soon," like they were in cahoots. So, I stayed.

Then, at Pua's funeral, I went out with Rell and Dave in the four-man canoe. After the funeral, when they committed her ashes to the sea, I jumped in the water and felt her presence. I'm really far from shore at this point. I felt this buoyancy. I swam to shore, and they went back in the canoe. It took me a long time, but I just swam and just, somehow, felt maybe what it was that they felt when they were out there—a kind of buoyancy and comfort that I had never felt before.

A Fair Trade ⟩ Dennis Pang

THE FURTHEST BACK I can remember Rella, it was prior to her being sponsored by any surfboard company. I used to drive out from my house in Niu Valley to see her at the Mākaha International contest. Martha was actually the star of the family back then; she even went on to the world championships.

I met Rell in '66 and '67, and she really liked the boards I made. So, she used to have her boyfriend then, Jeff, tune up my Volkswagen Bug as trade for a board from me. There was no money exchanged because she had no money.

Whenever she needed a board, she would have her boyfriend do work on my car. I was kind of her first sponsor.

Eventually, she got involved with Local Motion and Robbie Burns from Kailua, and I was just a small-change shaper. But, she really loved my boards way back then.

Bird of Prey Gets Grounded ⟩ Dennis Pang

I WAS SURFING Threes one time, and it was a pretty good day. But, this really ferocious-looking guy was ripping me off wave after wave. I didn't know him, but I knew who he was. It was Bird Mahelona, and he was "the man" at Mākaha back in the early '70s—a brilliant surfer, but a really tough customer.

He preceded Johnny Boy Gomes, and, in fact, Johnny Boy emulated him. Bird has this big birthmark on his forehead, and Johnny Boy cut his forehead so he could look fierce like Bird. He was revered and feared at the same time. And he was burning me at Threes…burning me and everybody else big time. But, I didn't want to say anything.

Then, Rell paddles out, and she paddles up to me, gets off her board, and gives me a hug and a kiss in the water.

I started talking to her, and I said "That's Bird, right? He's snatching all the waves from everybody."

She said "I'll talk to him."

And I said, "Nah, nah, don't do it."

But she goes over and talks to him, and, after that, the guy let me have waves. She totally neutralized the situation. He was burning guys right and left and she went over and calmed him down. In typical "Rell" fashion, she solved the problem.

She was the queen of Mākaha even way back then. She was just awesome. The true meaning of Hawaiian *aloha* emanated from her.

She used to take Chinese food to the lifeguard headquarters at Kapiʻolani Park and feed them all. If you were to have any kind of role model, it would be Rell Sunn in terms of the *aloha*… the giving…the purity of it all. Get off her board and give you a hug and a kiss in the water. Nobody does that.

Ride the Mild Surf 〈 Tara Torburn

WE HAD MADE plans that on this trip that Rell was going to take me out to Baby Queens and teach me how to surf, right where the beach boys stash their boards. On that particular trip, the cancer had spread to her lungs. We picked her up at the doctor's office where they had confirmed what she had suspected for a long time.

This was couple days before Thanksgiving, and we had the Menehune Contest to do. When we got home, she made arrangements to fly to Chicago for a medical protocol. She came back on Thanksgiving, and I cooked Thanksgiving dinner at her house. We had the three days of the Menehune Contest then went to the Eddie Aikau contest press conference. After that, we drove to her little, secret, free parking place near the Duke statue. She took our photos with the Duke statue. Then, she went and grabbed a board from the Kūhiō Beach surfboard racks and said, "This is the board I wanted to take out with you. I'm glad it's here." There was no

Pictured above: Kathy Terada.

one in the little rental shack, so she tells us to put our stuff in the sand beneath the booth.

We take our board out, surf, throw the *lei* in the water, the full routine. Even in spite of all of her cancer, I think she was more excited about getting me out there than I was.

The surf was small, and she and Dan are standing out in the water. I'm scared to death, and I'm going, "Oh, my god! I'm going! I'm going!"

I could have sworn I was standing up straight, but the photo proved I wasn't.

We came in and got our bags. She tried to give the beach boy money, but he said, "Oh, Rell, no way." She used Dan's water camera to take our Christmas card photos with Diamond Head in the background, me on the board, and Dan holding me up over his head. It is one of my favorite photos…a photo by Rell.

Flowing with the Spirit ⟩ Fred Hemmings

WITH RELL HAVING left us now, I often wonder how she endured so long with the terrible disease and the hardships she was going through. This story relates to what her real strength was in many ways—the strength of her spirit.

Back in the early days of professional surfing and surfing on network television before cable, I was producing an event for ABC Wide World of Sports—a tandem surfing event. They chose Rell to do the commentating alongside myself, and, then, of course, the anchor commentator, who was Bill Flemming at that time with ABC.

The waves are about three to four feet at Mākaha and just perfect for tandem surfing—one of those beautiful days of bright sun and clean environment…the wonderful ocean. Rell and I are standing there with the director of the show, who is, of course, from Manhattan in New York City and knows absolutely zero about surfing. He wants us to go out and catch a wave. I'm supposed to pick Rell up, put her on my shoulders, and ride up to the beach; then, jump off the board, run up to the camera, and introduce ourselves and welcome the audience to the event.

Well, that's obviously easier said than done. Catching a wave on cue and riding it up to the beach and jumping off and running up to a microphone could be very difficult. You could do it ten times and not get it right. So, we paddled out on the tandem board, and, on the way out, I found out how strong Rell's spirit is.

I had assumed that I knew a little bit about surfing and certainly had been tandem surfing before, but I guess Rell didn't make that assumption. Right from the time we got on the board, she took command and control of everything. "Paddle here; paddle there; line up here; sit there. Okay, here's the wave. Start paddling, Fred. Now, pick me up, Fred. Okay, let's start riding, Fred."

She was in total control the whole way just through. And the funny part about it was a wave came along and we got the cue from the director on the beach. We caught it and rode all the way up to the beach, got off the board, ran up to the camera, and did the whole thing in one take. It was quite an experience, and the only thing I can say is that it was done only because of Rell's absolutely incredible willpower and the strength of her spirit.

I think that is probably what served her so well in her life and made her such a dominant person in the surfing culture we all enjoy.

The Wāhine Take Over 〉 Glen Moncata

RELL HAD ALWAYS wanted a women's contest at Māhaka. But, you know the politics out there—it's a men's contest. "This is a man's way. You can't do this."

So, once again, she drove from Māhaka to Kailua (and this was when she was very ill). She sat down and said, "Now that you guys have Roxy, my vision is to put on a big event just like Buff's but for women only."

"Oh, gosh, how am I going to do that?"

"You can figure it out."

"Thanks a lot, Rell."

We decided to do it. And, during the planning, she got very ill. So, she went to the mainland for one of her cancer treatments, and we put the contest together. But, in Rell's absence, we were kind of concerned. So, I called her and told her, "You know, Rell, we've got this contest that you wanted for two days. Are enough girls going to come out?"

"You put on the contest; the girls will show up."

"Fine. Whatever you want."

So, we had three divisions: longboard, shortboard, and bodyboard. She had called me from

Houston or wherever she was, asking me, "How is the contest going?"

"Don't worry about the contest; worry about you."

"I'm fine. I'm fine. Is the contest on? I'm coming home on Thursday, and I don't know if I'm going to be able to surf in it."

"Whatever you want to do. We'll pick you up. We'll take you to the beach. We'll do whatever you want."

Two days before the contest, she came home…very weak and very ill.

The day of the contest arrived, and we had about sixty entries. Little did we know there would be another one-hundred girls on the beach wanting to enter the contest. It became the first Rell Sunn Roxy Jam. We had one-hundred-and-seventy-five women in that contest. It was unheard of in those days. In most of the other women's contests in all the years we ran those events, if we could fill two heats we were happy.

On contest morning, Rell came down to the beach and said, "I'm feeling a little tired, but I'll paddle out and ride a wave to open the contest and see how I feel."

So, Auntie Momi gave the blessing, and Rell went out, with hundreds of people on the beach. Of course, the day before, the surf was bumpy and lumpy. But, the contest day turned out to be one of the classic days at Mākaha—three to four feet and absolutely glassy, not a breath of wind.

Rell took off on this wave and just looked like the queen of Mākaha—just perfect. She made a bottom turn and walked to the nose…did the whole thing. She came in, and everybody cheered, and she said, "I'm entering the contest." She entered all three divisions, won two of them, and became the iron woman of the contest.

Still Surfing with Rell ⟩ Sonja Evensen

WHENEVER I GET a really good wave, still to this day, that's when I feel Rell. I think, "God, I wish I could move like her." When I get a super good wave, it's like, "Wow! Rell!" It's just like she's right with me. That's like the closest place I can be with her.

She started me off at Queens and Threes in Waikīkī, so it was pretty manageable. As a sail-boarder, it's not like I had a huge amount of fear. It's just that I didn't know how to "surf" surf.

Really soon after, she made me enter Buff's contest, and I didn't know what I was doing. But, I was a gymnast, and, so, I did like Scooter Boy, and I got some sort of prize for it.

But, she pushes you. She's like, "I've got a board for you. Just do it."

And I go, "Okay." I didn't know any better.

Then, there were big waves, and she'd tell me where to sit because she was so confident about it. I knew enough about waves to know if I were in any trouble or not. But, there was never any of this, "You can't," which is the same thing she did for the kids.

That's what I was watching, especially with the Menehune kids. The kids would light up because she paid attention to them and noticed what good stuff they did. It meant so much to them that she saw them. It was confidence building.

I wanted to tap into that in a big way, and I helped start an ocean program in Waimānalo, *Hui Malama o ke Kai*. It's because I saw Rell do that with kids in Mākaha. I thought, "I can take some kids in Waimānalo." It's an after-school program. It was based on what I saw Rell do. My vision came from Rell. I thought, "There is something to this, where kids maybe aren't doing well in school and they weren't really connecting." But, the ocean had that. I think that's the whole thing about her taking them to France and getting them that exposure. I feel that's part of getting kids to connect to something.

It's like her thing with the tide pools. Really look at it and see how fascinating the world is. How many kids did she get all fascinated by *limu*?! It's just that fascination with everything and getting kids jazzed about stuff. She just had that kid-like quality that says you should just have fun.

Pua's Wave Blessing ⟩ Luana Froiseth

ONE DAY, it was kind of weird. We were out surfing, and our friend Pua Moku'au had passed away. We always surfed for so long that the surf would come up. It would be two feet when we started, and, by the time we came in, it was ten feet.

So, on this day, we had just started surfing. It was about three to four feet, more on the three side than the four. We started talking about Pua, and Rell said, "You know, Pua is out here surfing with us."

I said, "Yeah. But, you know, Pua likes to surf bigger waves than over here. It's a little bit small for Pua."

All of a sudden, a huge set comes in, and we scattered. Then, it goes to nothing. So, we're sitting out there again, waiting for another wave to come in. There are only four of us out there, and it's glassy—perfect conditions. We're talking about Pua again, and another big set comes in.

After the session was over, the waves came down to about three feet again. I said to Rell, "Ho, where did those waves come from? Maybe we should talk about Pua more often. We should try that at another break."

And Rell said, "Nah, it's not gonna work. It's only gonna work at Mākaha."

Rell's 'Ohana

Just Follow the Leader ⟩ Bernie Baker

YVON CHOUINARD invited us on a trip to Christmas Island that was four parts adventure and two parts surf because that's what Christmas Island is—a classic atoll sitting in the middle of the Pacific.

When we came up from the airport on the other side of the island to the house we were going to stay in, we were sort of like going, "Okay, we've got Yvon and Rell and Dave Parmenter and Sam George and myself. How are we going to divide this whole thing up? Who's going to go in which room?"

I think Rell had already chosen her room based upon the light coming through the window. She liked the way it shined through this one room. It might have reminded her of her bedroom at Mākaha. There was a certain look to it. These were pretty minimal rooms, just bunk beds, nothing on the wall. But, she knew that was her bedroom and us three guys could fight over the others.

Christmas Island doesn't have a Polynesian feel or any kind of romantic look. It really is just a couple feet above sea level. The funny thing is that, because it's world famous for its bonefishing, very few people have gone there specifically to go surfing.

You have to wait on the swell because you need the surf in Hawai'i to be fifteen feet to get four and five foot surf on Christmas Island. But the lack of surf didn't bother Rell.

I remember how she would see something—it might have been a grove of palm trees that was a couple hundred yards away from our little home in the village of London [Ronton, Kiribati]. She would see it and rally the troops. She was always really good at rallying the troops, getting everybody together and getting them all enthused saying, "We should check that thing out." I was really surprised she didn't drag us over to check out a can on the road or something. But, that was Rell's personality. She could get you to go and do something completely against whatever else it was you were going to do just because she could create this level of interest and mystery in something she had seen.

You had to go. That was it. You had to go. Rell came up with an idea, she put together a package, and everyone else was up and running.

There were a few rusted-out hulls of small boats that have not held up through the years in the lagoon right by the dock, and she would be checking out all the little nooks and crannies and portholes and the rusted bow and all that kind of stuff. She had that curiosity in her that made it so interesting to spend a day, a week, a month, or whatever with her because she was always looking for what's inside of something.

It was classic when she went bonefishing because she's not a fly fisherman per se. Obviously, her forte growing up in Hawai'i, like most kids, is spearfishing. Grab a mask, grab a snorkel, grab a spear, get in the water. Yet, there she was, out there. I remember the first day we decided to go over to the bonefishing flats and practice in a nice, flat, sandbar area.

Rell was all decked out with her sunglasses and her big bonnet, all covered up against the sun. Yvon took her out into the waist-deep water to have her whip back and forth in classic fly fishing style, and she quickly got the hang of it. If she had never sewn in her life and somebody handed her a sewing machine and just sort of showed her how you run the needle and the

foot pedal, it wouldn't take her long to learn it. So, she was out there pretty quick, and she was pretty hooked. She was watching the whole thing, how you could see the fish cruising in the flat water, which is what you have to look for with polarized sunglasses, and, boy, she was on it. She was like "Miss Bonefish." That was Yvon's main reason for going there, to go bonefishing, and everything else was pretty much icing on the cake. So, as much as Sam and Dave and I were focused on surfing, Yvon had brought the gear down and everybody had to do their duty and go bonefishing with him.

The explorer inside her kept her wound up. So, anytime she saw anything along the sandy road or maybe across the lagoon, she was always, "If only we could get a boat to check that out."

We went over to a little atoll called Cook Island. It's a bird sanctuary, and it's right on the edge of the entrance into the lagoon in the village of London. We all loaded into this boat with Charlie Corben, who was down there at the time having married a woman from Tarawa, the capital of Kiribati. It was really neat because we went cruising around Cook Island and checked out all the birds and the nests with all the eggs. And, boy, Rell was on it. You've got to realize, Rell was part ornithologist and part marine biologist and part starfish hunter—anything and everything, especially if it involves the ocean. I don't think there was a tide pool at that end of Christmas Island that she didn't inspect during the week that we were there. Everything held endless fascination for her. She was constantly inspecting every little nook and cranny for anything that had some sort of exploration value in it.

The house where we stayed was owned by the government. It was probably the only rental in the community, and you had to go through an agency to get a reservation. It was built really well—a concrete block type home. Government officials would stay in it where they were in town. There was a little customs department in a cottage that was only open when large vessels called in ahead of time to say that they were going to anchor outside and bring in supplies for the village. There was a communications building that had satellite phone service, when it was working, and couple of big satellite dishes outside. You had a store for everybody who lives there because it's the second-largest village on the island.

To us guys, all those things were, "There's a store there and a phone room over there and stuff." But, not to Rell.

She goes, "Oh, no, no, no. We've really got to go see the town."

We go, "Town? What town?"

She asks, "What are all those buildings?"

I think the whole time we were there we saw maybe twenty people at the most.

But, Rell just goes, "Let's go check that out. Let's go walking down there."

And we're thinking, "Oh, god. In the heat of the morning?"

Everybody, especially the locals, are tucked away for the next few hours. But, there we were, all dressed up in long-sleeve shirts and sun visors flopping around this town. I'm sure everybody was looking out from their little houses going, "What the hell are they doing?" It gets hot down there after eight-thirty or nine o'clock. You can feel it. The trade winds blow, and they're really hot, humid trade winds coming off the water.

But there's Rell checking out the store and the communications place, checking out this and checking out that. It was classic because the customs cottage was locked up ninety percent of the time. Yet, there she was, looking through the little window with the metal bars. She was looking at everything, just snooping around. Curiosity once again.

Regarding Dave, I thought that was the first time there was a really close friendship beginning to bloom between the two of them at a guy/girl level. I noticed in their conversation they were very, very much in tune with what interested the other party. What Dave found interesting, Rell held interesting, and what Rell thought was worthy of extended conversation, Dave got into it. It was sort of a natural between the two of them that definitely clicked on that friendship level as far as interests go. I mean, Dave is a superb waterman and Rell being the princess in the ocean. Anything that interested her, that was ocean oriented, they were off and running with it. He sort of kept an eye on her, and, if she came up with a good idea and nobody else wanted to share in it, he would say, "Hey, I'll go with you."

There was a guy down there who had the only skindiving business in the area, and the diving is obviously phenomenal because you don't have any other divers and it's really untouched. This American guy had this neat little grass shack kind of shop. We had met him on the street in town one day, and he wanted to know all about us and what we were doing. He invited us to come over to his business, which was a combination of dive shop downstairs and home upstairs. It was really funny because, the moment we went in, there Rell was ready to see how he lived, ready to see how things were set up, ready to check the whole situation.

Fortunately, he was a very cordial gentleman and he said, "Go ahead. The kitchen is over to the right," and she was on it. She wanted to see exactly how the whole layout was. It just a part of Rell. It was like she had to touch everything once, and, then, she was ready to go. She needed to connect with those things that held her curiosity. She needed to somehow physically or emotionally touch them at least once.

It's like a kid who says, "Okay, been there; done that." It was almost as though Rell was constantly seeing whether she could live in that situation, or if this could hold her curiosity for more than just a moment where she could, then, become a part of it.

Friends at First Sight ⟨ Jeannie Chesser

I MET RELL at Mākaha when I first came to Hawai'i in 1971. I was a budding photographer and had an eight-hundred millimeter lens, and I was taking pictures all over. I took some pictures of Rell surfing at Mākaha in some kind of contest. She had gotten third or fourth place, and I just went up to her and said, "Oh, my god! You surfed so much better than the other girls."

We became friends instantly. I was living on the North Shore, then Kailua for awhile. But, I was always driving around. I went to Mākaha a lot because we both had our kids who were just a month in age apart. Jan is a January baby, and Todd is a February baby. We had a lot in common.

We were both single mothers, and a couple years went by and we started going out with these guys who were best friends. Me and Rell and them just became a tight-knit little group. We'd go out and do stuff, go to movies, everything was so fun and carefree back then. We'd go surfing, of course. I wasn't as good a surfer as she was. But, she would always encourage me and always point out all the good things about yourself.

I would go to Mākaha a lot. I liked hanging out, and it was fun to be with Rell. Neither of us had any money, but neither one of us worked too much for some reason.

We brought the kids to let them play on the beach. They also were in preschool, so we would surf and go back to our homes by the time they got out of school. There's a lot of time Jan would stay with us because she was boarding at Kamehameha Schools. When Rell would go on a trip or something, Jan would stay with us. She and Todd just had a blast. We never fantasized that they would grow up and get married. They were just buddies, and Jan outgrew him by at least two heads.

When Rell first went on the pro tour, I was kind of like, "Hey, I want to go, too." But, Rell had a way better chance than me, so it was kind of understood that she would go and I would stay behind. She went to China and Japan and South Africa and all over the world. She would always bring me something back because she was a perpetual shopper.

Living on Rell Time ⟩ Jeannie Chesser

EARLY ON, I had a boat in the Ala Wai Harbor. We'd go down there and meet and go surfing. I rented a house in Kailua, but I lived on the boat because I loved that wave at Ala Moana, and I had an opportunity to buy this funky little boat. I paid two-thousand dollars, and the slip was twenty-four dollars…the second one from the end.

So, Rell would tell me, "Okay, I'm coming down, and I'm going to meet you to go surfing."

So, I'd sit there and I'd wait. Ten o'clock would come; eleven o'clock would come; twelve o'clock would come, and she wouldn't show up. Sometimes it would even be the next day before I'd hear from her. And she would act like it never happened. I'd be all, "What happened? Where were you? I was waiting for hours for you."

And she'd say, "Oh, something came up." So, from that very day I knew—don't wait for someone on land; always wait for someone in the water.

To this day, I tell people, "I'll meet you at the beach, but I'll be in the water. If you want me to come in, just stand on the rocks and call." So, that was one very good lesson I learned from Rell. That was "Rell Time."

Puka Shell Madness ⟩ Jeannie Chesser

WE WERE REALLY into *puka* shelling, this was when you could go up to 'Ehukai Beach with a bucket and fill it. You just scoop. There was no sand; it was all *puka* shells. There was this one time that the surf at Mākaha was flat, and we had the little fish scoop nets. You could scoop from the bottom of the ocean, and you'd get so many and just pull it up and pour it in the bucket.

So, the very first time, we were out not too far. You didn't have to dive deep. Rell said, "Okay, I'm going to dive down and get the shells, and you stay on top and watch for sharks."

And I was just, "What? I didn't know that was my job? What the hell? You never told me that was my duty."

It was only us out there; the beaches weren't crowded. We used to go to Mākua Cove. There was nobody around…nobody. Now that I think of it, it was kind of dangerous. But it was beautiful down there.

We were always looking for shells, and, one time, we said, "All right, we're going to Sunset Beach to surf." We pull up and could park right there at the point. Then, we walked back a little bit because we wanted to look at the waves. We checked it out and went, "Yeah, it looks like it's only about four to six feet…really perfect, offshore winds, only a few guys out."

So, we're walking on the beach, and we see this frickin' gigantic set, like twelve feet, just cleaning up everybody. People are throwing their boards. It's just pandemonium everywhere.

Both of us, at the exact same time, while we're walking to get our boards, went, "Oh, maybe we'll just look for shells." And both our heads pointed straight down to the sand. So, we didn't go out that day, just kind of walked around looking for shells. I can still picture this one red board, a pintail, and this guy just throwing his board and the spray going off. It was crazy.

We used to have so much fun at Chun's. Every Easter, the Chun's surf meet would be on, so we would have an Easter egg hunt for the kids. We'd hide Easter eggs on the beach and stuff, and they'd find 'em. It was great. We'd do the same thing at Mākua Cove—just hide 'em in the reef and in the little tide pools.

Fortune Favors the Bold 〉 Luana Froiseth

RELL AND I used to pick up all kinds of stuff at the Salvation Army, Goodwill, places like that. So, we go over there, and Rell says, "I'm looking for ten cushions for my rattan set."

"Ten cushions? We're never going to find ten cushions in one place. Are you crazy or what?"

She goes, "Yeah, yeah, yeah. We will; we will."

So, we start at the Salvation Army up by my house. I say, "I don't see any cushions."

She says, "I don't see any either. Let's go look in the back." So, we go in the employees-only area, she opens the curtain, and, lo and behold, there are ten cushions over there.

I go, "I can't believe this."

She goes, "Ten cushions! Where's the manager? I want to buy them."

The manager comes and says to her, "You look familiar."

I whisper to Rell, "This is your chance, Rell. Go for it, and get the lowest price you can get."

So, she tells the manager, "I want to buy these cushions."

"How much do you want to pay?"

"I only want to pay twenty-five bucks."

My eyes open wide and I think, "What? Twenty five bucks for ten cushions? That's crazy."

And the manager goes, "Okay, you can have them."

People recognizing her would do anything for her. Rell really never got paid a bit of money to be a surfing athlete. But, people would go out of their way for her, even people who didn't know her but who had heard of her.

We would go to restaurants, and they'd go, "Oh, Rell, let me get you some of this and some of that."

And I'd say, "This is working well."

Yet, when she was being interviewed by somebody, she would pinpoint the restaurants that had helped her. She would always give back to you what you gave to her.

Name Games ⟩ Sweets

"RELLA PROPELLA." She had that name from when she was in high school. My name is Sweets, but I was born with that name. So, when you have names like "Sweets" and "Rell," you know you're going to have kids teasing you.

So, one day, she and I sat down. It was so cute. She was remembering, "Geez, Sweets, when you was in school, you had a lot of nicknames?"

And I said, "Oh, Rell, you not going believe the names I had—'Sweets,' 'Spareribs,' all kind of names."

And she said, "Mine was 'Rella Propella.'"

So, every time I called her, I'd say, "Yo, Propells."

And she'd say, "Yo, Ribs."

Lovely Little Hula Hands ⟩ Jim Kempton

RELL USED TO have these Thanksgiving dinners that we went to for years. It was right when we would come over for the Triple Crown of Surfing. So, she had this big *kālua* turkey thing she would do.

One year, this big Hawaiian guy was there playing guitar. My daughter, who was about three years old then, was captivated by his music. She had skin as white as skin gets, and bright red hair. We had bought her this little hula outfit, the kind of thing you get in Waikīkī, and we had it in the car.

So, this guy is sitting on Rell's front porch, and my daughter is watching him play, and, all of a sudden, she turned around and ran down the steps, opened the car door, and got out her hula costume. I don't know if she'd ever seen hula before. But, she puts this outfit on, and she walks out in front of him. She's not really doing the hula but putting her hand on her hip and sort of dancing in the way a kid at three would dance.

He just flipped, and he started playing everything.

Rell came out and said, "Jim, Jim, take a picture."

And I said, "I don't want to spoil this."

So, Rell goes, "That's Henry Kapono. Do you know who this is?"

It was just a fun thing, just as all of Rell's Thanksgiving dinners were.

An Urgency for Hawaiian Culture
Kanani Amu Kamahele

I USED TO live right next door to Rell, but I didn't really grow up out here like Rell did. I grew up in Lā'ie, and I used to go surfing and diving with my boy cousins. My dad was a fisherman. He worked at Pearl Harbor, but, every spare moment, we were fishing.

The laws of fishing have changed, but, before, we used to fish with *moi* nets all night. We'd get up at five in the morning and pick up the nets before the sun hit them. If the net was caught on the reef, we'd have to dive to free it. So, my dad taught me how to dive. We picked *limu* and *'opihi*. We did a lot of things that, until I grew up, I didn't know how "cultural" they were. It was just part of our life. But, in the late '70s, there was an urgency for a lot of us who were young Hawaiians to know more than just our foods. Our *kupuna* were not allowed to speak their language, and, when you lose your language, you lose your culture.

There was an urgency. Things were happening. They were bombing Kaho'olawe, and some of the people who lived on Moloka'i and Maui thought that was wrong. From their homes, they could watch this special island being destroyed. That's where the Hawaiian navigators had been trained. From that point, you can get to Tahiti—the distant homeland. There are just a lot of cultural things that, through the years, were lost and just not known. And, for us dancing hula, things that are not known were spooky. Before our dance, we'd pray. But, when we'd dance about Pele and about Kamapua'a and the *ali'i* and commoners, we didn't pray to them. A lot of us are Christians, so we thought we would get zapped. But, we still wanted to know about our culture.

When we went to hula, I'd retain things well. When we were taught a song, we'd have to know the meaning of the words and where it came from. It would come really easy for me, and I'd always get one-hundred percent. I started talking to my grandma because I was going to college. She used to tell me stories about Kahoʻolawe. She used to stay there because she was a cousin to Jonah Kūhiō Kalanaianaʻole, who was our first delegate to Washington. She hung out with his wife, and they used to stay in Waikīkī when there were taro patches, and the pier would go out into the ocean, and there were houses at the end. That's why it's called Kūhiō Beach [named after the Kūhiō *ʻohana*].

Little things like that, to me, were great things because I didn't know. In that urgency, Auntie Maʻiki graduated lots of young *kumu hula*. Most *kumu* don't. For all of us who were hungry, young Hawaiians, we joined these *hālau*. They became great, big *hālau*, and big competitions followed. It was through that urgency for us to learn more that we learned how to make our instruments from raw materials and not just from the hula supply store. We learned how to make our *lei*; we went to the mountain to gather materials. We learned what was symbolic for this person or that person; we learned that the *kukui* was a *kinalau*, or plant form, of the demigod Kamapuaʻa and why. *Kukui* is symbolic of wisdom. So, when somebody graduates, you want to give him a *lei* like that.

Rell, a young Hawaiian woman, was looking for the same thing. She went to Kamehameha Schools. Kamehameha is one of the elite schools, and I'm sure Rell learned a lot of things at Kamehameha. They really teach you to get out in the real world. They're still cultural, but Rell was like us—hungry to learn more. She joined the *hālau*, too. But, we never realized how much we already knew.

When me and Rell would go diving, we'd put our *limu* bags on our backs and go to Mākaha beach and pick *limu*. She'd go diving, and we'd make raw fish and eat our *limu*. But, today, no more *limu* at Mākaha. And people don't know how to pick *limu* anymore. They pull it up from the roots, and it kills it.

Rell and I got close. It was funny—I never told anybody I used to make her *lei*. She would always have to do something. She'd say, "I've gotta go; I'm not gonna come back." And we'd be going into a show or a competition, so I'd make them for her.

I always thought she was great because she lived in two worlds and tried to blend them together. She would bring a lot of friends into this world, and they loved it. They never wanted to leave her house.

Lots of *haole* boys used to fall in love with her, but I think she always wanted to have a local boy. She was a beautiful Hawaiian. I don't know how really close she was to her family because they never visited. I think they finally recognized how great she was later. They're all great in their own way. She has beautiful sisters and a brother. But, it's like she did it all on her own.

The guys were great to her. Uncle Buff, Uncle Homer—they respected her. She was a respectful person to everybody as well, even kids. The kids really loved her. She loved everybody.

You couldn't go down the road without, every other minute, somebody tooting or waving.

We'd go to town, and I'd say, "Girl, I tell you…*Miss Aloha*." She just knew everybody.

But, she still would say, "Come on over. Come on. Let's have some coffee." She knew I didn't drink coffee, so she'd make me tea.

And she loved to eat. Even though she shouldn't have the butter, she'd just pour it on her mango bread.

I remember she'd pick *'aloe*…peel it off and eat all the insides and, then, drink orange juice. And I'd think, "Oh, my god, girl." But, she was into the herbal healing. She was totally cultural, yet she could be in the western world. That was because she was so open and she invited everybody into both worlds.

We went out diving at Mākaha together. First, we picked *limu*, and it was just a great diving day. She came up with *uhu*, and we had a great meal after that. She was so quick. She's gone there so many times that she knew exactly where the fish live. So, she'd go to their home and get *anykine*.

She'd surf at night, every full moon. She'd dawn patrol in the morning and, then, come back at night and say, "Come on, girlfriend. Wake up. Let's go." She fit so many things in one day. "We can do it. We can do it. And we'll come back, and we'll visit." But, totally taking no breaks. Just go, go, go.

She didn't really quit hula, but she'd always have to go on trips. She'd always have to leave, and she'd always come back. But, her daughter always stayed. I know Jan was always at hula on Saturdays because, when my *kumu hula* would go on trips, I'd be the teacher.

Pua Moku'au was my best friend. We grew up together. I have pictures of me and Rell and Pua in our hula garb. Pua lasted about six months, and Rell was the last one. They're both gone. I think it was a cultural gathering of the three of us. In our quest for our culture, we looked for it in hula. Me and Rell kind of understood that, even though we didn't know a lot and were still learning. We were already doing a lot in our culture…food-wise, gathering-wise, the ocean. We were surrounded by the ocean, and you gotta know your ocean. I'm happy that we got to spend that time because, after a while, I moved down the street, and we didn't get to spend much time together. Life was different, and she would be going out to different places around the world surfing. But, I got to see lot of her daughter.

Rell was always giving. A lot of people came to her house, but not a lot would go in her bedroom. I would go in her room to talk story, and she would say, "Here, I have something for you. You should have this." (Some Hawaiian, silk shirt that I still have.) She would always be giving me stuff, just sharing everything.

She was a lifeguard, and Pua was, too. After a car broke my leg, they would bury me in the sand, and I would have to dig myself out without using my hands. They would make me paddle a boogie board two-and-a-half miles every day.

They were the enforcers. I'm like, "No more!"

And they're all, "Come on!" They had so much energy. I don't know where they got it from.

Rell lasted a long time, and probably a lot of it she was suffering. But, Pua shocked us. We were at hula, and I got a phone call from Butch. Pua had been at the hospital, and she had just passed away. We were practicing because we knew it was going to be our last trip together. But, because Pua was such a loving person, I honestly believe she had to go that way. She had to go very quickly, since she was so happy…never suffering. It was so like her to just go. I was shocked. I wrote a song for her. She was the mediator, and she always tried to be cupid, hooking up somebody with somebody else, trying to make things good. For her to suffer, it was just not her. So, when she went so quickly, I was really thankful that I got to spend her last six months with her. It was so like her not to burden anybody else.

I miss them terribly. Once in a while driving a car I drop a tear, but I know they're in a greater place.

Truly, I think that our cultural urgency helped us see where everybody else was at. A lot of us were asking questions. I went into Hawaiian studies because I didn't know enough about our culture. I needed to know. There are more young people speaking Hawaiian now than older people. I never had children, so I wasn't able to pass on anything that I know to them. But, I've taught thousands of people in my time, and now I teach adults Hawaiiana.

That was what kept us bonded. We grew up differently, but we understood the ocean. I always thought Rell was one of the more intelligent local girls. She expressed herself well and was a great organizer. She wasn't afraid. A lot of Hawaiians will sit in the back of the room and not ask any questions. Rell was one of the ones who sat in front of the class and asked all kinds of questions. I learned a lot from her.

I remember we would come out from the ocean and put all our gear away or just sit down and have a drink under that same *kamani* tree at Mākaha. The kids would come by, and she would make them pick up rubbish before they went in the water. She would talk to them, and they'd go, "Okay, auntie."

They'd clean up the beach, and they would go in the water, and she'd go and play with them. She was great that way…just great. They would have so much awe for her that they'd go, "Whatever you say, auntie. How far you like me dive down?"

An Ocean Dancer ︶ Kathy Terada

JAN WAS THE better dancer. Jan was the one who could remember. Jan would sit and watch our class, and, if we couldn't remember something when we would get together to practice, Jan would always remember. Jan could always tell us, "Oh, it goes like this."

I don't think it was important to Rell to be the best dancer.

I've read what a beautiful, graceful dancer she was. But she wasn't that good of a hula dancer. It's because she danced in the surf. I don't think she could be as graceful anywhere else like she was when she surfed.

I mean, when you watched her ride the waves, she danced. She was so smooth and so graceful, but you put her on land and she wasn't.

So, I called my friend Kanani (Amu) because I didn't know how Rell ended up in Mili's *hālau*. Amu said that near the end of the '70s was the first time that to be Hawaiian and to learn Hawaiian things was a good thing. She said that, for them, there was this urgency to learn. Some of them, like Pua and Amu, had grown up dancing in studios. In the studios it was hula, but it was *hapa haole* hula. They mixed in Tahitian and Maori, and it was Polynesian dance—kind of for show.

But, for the first time, after Auntie Ma'iki graduated her students, it was more than just hula. It was *kahiko*; it was chanting. It was the language and the culture and the history of the land. Amu said Mili was in Wai'anae, so they went there. Amu became a Hawaiian language teacher, and, for the first time, you learned the history.

When we studied with Mili, we would have to learn the words to the song and learn the translation and, then, whatever the place name was or the person who the song was about or the chant was written about. We had to research. We had to write papers and document where the research came from. And, then, we were tested. So, like Amu said, she really learned all that, and she took it further and went back to school to study.

Amu told me something that she thought was really special about Rell. Amu's family all lived in town, grew up in town. They would come out here because they had grandparents or family who lived out here. They would run away to here to escape the city. And, when she met Rell, Rell lived this life. She did everything that they came out to experience and to learn. Amu couldn't believe that Rell knew all these things. And, for Rell, because she lived everything that was Hawaiian and traditional, hula was just another part of it.

But she didn't put a lot of effort into it. She was not a line dancer. I always remember her a little bit behind everybody so she could use her peripheral vision. But, she wasn't real discreet about that, either. And she was always a little bit off because she was following, yeah? But she still loved it, and she brought energy to the class.

Art from the Heart ⟩ Fletcher Chouinard

I GOT INJURED snowboarding once. I broke my back, and I was kind of laid up. It was about the same time Rell was really sick, and she got a hold of this butcher paper, or huge scratch-pad paper, three feet by three feet, and wrote this huge, long, double-sided letter on this enormous butcher paper. It was like, probably, eight sheets of paper—an enormous work of art. She drew all kinds of pictures and diagrams, and it was like this big motivational "pick yourself back up regardless of the outcome," "things will be fine as long as you don't give up."

She was so sick at that point that I had no idea how she had the energy to do such a thing. She couldn't surf. She was just pretty much sitting around the house…couldn't do anything else. It's amazing to me. It's something that would have been an undertaking for me being completely healthy to write something like that. And it was incredibly creative; it wasn't just motivational workshop kind of stuff. There were all kinds of drawings all over it and everything. I keep it in a fireproof box. I don't really know what else to do with it. It's double sided; I can't frame it. I go look at it every once in a while.

It blew my mind when I got it. I couldn't believe it. I opened it up. (It was all folded up, so it looked small but thick, and I kept unfolding and unfolding.) It was massive. I went, "Oh, my god." It wasn't so much a letter as it was a present. It's probably the most valuable thing I have. It's amazing. I did feel a little bit silly for feeling sorry for myself. It put things in perspective.

A lot of times there are people who have disappeared from your life for one reason or another, and you can't remember voices…how they sound. I totally can remember the way Rell would say anything. I can hear her voice in my head. I've thought about that a lot. I can't remember what my grandparents' voices sounded like, but I can remember Rell's completely clearly.

The Sunn and the Moon After Midnight
Brickwood Galuteria

ONE STORY THAT is very prominent in my history with Rell was something my kids will never forget—when we used to go moonlight surfing with Auntie Rell. She'd call me or I'd call her when it was full moon, and, maybe about one or two o'clock in the morning, depending on how the surf conditions were, when the moon was low and coming down already, a big, fat *manapua* up there. All of my kids would be ready just in case we got the call, and my nephews would come over to sleep. They were just beginning their surfing deal. Then, we would go down to meet Auntie Rell in Waikīkī. She used to bring a few boards, and we had boards, and we would meet where Duke's statue is today. We'd get the chili and rice going for when the kids would come in. We'd get some light tubes and crack 'em, and they'd light up, and we'd all wear them so we could find each other. We'd go out and go moonlight surfing and it was incredible…"mooning" each other, too.

That is something we'll never forget about Rell—not only her love of the ocean but her love of family and getting together. We had the Sunn and the moon all at the same time. It gave the kids a sense of adventure and something that they'll never forget for the rest of their lives—going moonlight surfing with Auntie Rell.

She was so encouraging and comforting to go out with in the ocean in the dark. I remember my nephew saying, "Oh, uncle. I scared; I scared."

And I said, "Come on. Let's go. Let's go. Auntie them are all out there waiting for us."

All my kids were out there. So, we got out there, and a couple of words of encouragement from the Queen of Mākaha, and that was it—everybody was on their way. A couple of adults and six kids out there, and Auntie Rell leading the way. There's nothing more safe than being out there with Auntie Rell.

Double Dose of Woe ⟩ Anona Napoleon

IN ONE CONTEST, as young women, we were all competing. Martha had won the Mākaha contest previously, and it was neat for me to be out there surfing with the Sunn sisters. During another contest at Mākaha, I dropped in on Rell. I hadn't seen her in the curl, and, all of a sudden, I noticed. "Oops! There she is coming up."

I had points deducted, and, when we went on the beach, I go, "I really didn't even see you."

She says, "That's okay. Let's go out and surf some more."

Years later, after she got her cancer, we were up on Moloka'i, and she and Ron Mizutani used to do commentary on the Moloka'i to O'ahu paddling competition. I was not really paddling.

I was an official because this was for the men's Moloka'i paddle.

So, Rell came by and said, "Eh, why don't you go with me down to the east end. They're having outdoor music."

I said, "Yeah, yeah." I just figured she'd jump in the car, and we'd go. But, here comes this limousine, and I said, "Oh, what is this? We're going in style."

Robyn Eastman, one of the DJs at KCCN radio, joined us. So, the three of us went to the east end, and we're sitting there listening to music and, all, of a sudden, Rell starts telling me she's having trouble with her marriage.

Robyn is sitting on my other side, and she says, "Yep, I'm having trouble with my marriage, too."

And, I'm thinking, "Oh, wow."

They say, "Could you just listen? We need to unload."

So, I say, "Okay."

I'm sitting there with these two women telling me their troubles.

I think that the great thing with Rell was that she didn't put on any pretenses. She was just a good, down-to-earth person.

Gifts from the Sea 〉 Tara Torburn

SOME OF THE things Rell would try to share with us, when we would stay with her, were from the time when she was a poor, single mom. When she had to give presents, she'd go down on the beach and find heart-shaped coral. Her driveway was full of them. We'd find the most miniature, ittiest, bittiest shells over by the blowhole at Mākaha, and we also did *limu* cards where we would go get the *limu*. Actually, she got the *limu* because I was too afraid to stand on the slippery, *limu*-covered rocks. We'd fill baggies with *limu* and arrange the *limu* and press the cards. We also did the fish prints. She'd find fish at the market with good eyes. Then, we'd try to make these nice fish cards and hand paint the eyes, but my eyes never came out any good.

Pieces of Rell 〉 Tara Torburn

WHEN RELL CAME to California and was staying in San Luis Obispo with Dave, we came to visit them. We would go to the coast, to Cambria and Cayucos, Morro Bay, and go shopping and antiquing. We went to a place that sold a lot of seashells, and she was buying abalone shells and things from the ocean.

I said, "You've got so many of these at your house."

She said, "Yeah, but everyone takes them."

Then, she started telling me something that I never had paid attention to—everybody thought she was rich. Because she was such a famous person, they thought she must be wealthy. She wasn't. I know she wasn't. She had medical bills. They latched onto her checking account and did all sorts of things. She was buying a lot of these abalone shells because she loved to put them all around her house. So, as the conversation progressed, I was amazed at how much she was spending on these things. I had never thought about how she came by them—maybe she found them or people gave them to her. Then, the conversation evolved to me saying, "You should put price tags on all the stuff in your house with a jar by the door so, when people leave, they know how much to put in."

People would just come in and take stuff from her—beach towels, Hawaiian clothes, her dresses. Her closets and drawers were packed so incredibly tight that she wouldn't miss something that was taken until she wanted it. Her little knickknacks and chotchkies—people would just take them. It was the downside of running Rell's "No-Tell Motel"…so many people coming and going. They wanted a part of her.

Egos and Appreciations ⟩ Tara Torburn

ONE TIME, Guy Motil, the surf photographer, was at Mākaha Beach, and we invited him for Thanksgiving dinner because he had no other plans. We were taking the turkey to Auntie Eileen's for a big Thanksgiving dinner. You are perpetually behind schedule when you're with Rell. You're never on time.

So, Rell told Guy, "You cut the turkey. Tara and I need to get dressed."

Guy's standing there going, "I can't believe I'm in Rell Sunn's kitchen carving the Thanksgiving turkey."

And at the same time, Rell is going, "I can't believe Guy Motil is in my kitchen carving the turkey."

I just told them, "You guys, enough with the mutual admiration. Let's get going."

A Real Working Vacation) Tara Torburn

WE HELPED RELL for five years with her Menehune Contest. The first year that we went over to help, she already had a lot of stuff underway. When she saw I knew how to set up the heats and do all the organizing stuff, she began waiting until I got there to get started setting up the contest.

Depending on my workload, we either came over the day before Thanksgiving or, if I were lucky, a couple days early. But, the contest always started on Friday. I'd get there, and she'd go, "Here's the applications and money."

"Do you know how many you have here?"

"No, you do that."

So, I'd sit and sort through everything. I spent all day and all night organizing heats with kids' names that I didn't know…trying to figure this out how many heats we were going to have… where the contest was actually going to be.

Rell would say, "I don't know. We might be over here or over there."

So, I'd try to organize everything in a very short period of time working on a computer that wasn't really good and trying to get her dot matrix printer to print things out. I would sort through the money to figure what we had, and, on top of all that, help cook Thanksgiving dinner because I was there to help and the contest started on Friday. If I were lucky, I'd have some time to spend afterward. But, it was good to feel needed.

Glen Moncata Miracle ⟩ Glen Moncata

'A'ohe hana nui, ke alu 'ia.
"No task is too big when done together by all."

WHEN WE HAD the funeral, I went a couple of days before to Buff and the boys, and I said, "Hey, what in the world are we going to do for parking out here?"

They said, "We don't know."

And I said, "Hey, look at this area here, the old parking lot. Can't we clean it up and park here."

"It gets too muddy." ("It gets this and it gets that.")

"Okay, guess what, guys. I'll figure out what to do. Let's clean this thing. I'll be out tomorrow afternoon."

So, I get out there, and here's all the boys with picks, shovels, and rakes trying to get the *kiawe* out of there and break it all down. We're sitting there and this kid comes up and says, "What are you guys doing."

I said, "We're clearing this lot because we need a parking lot for Auntie Rell's ceremony."
"Oh, maybe I can help."

"What do you got?"

"I can bring a dump truck over." So, ten minutes later, here comes a dump truck and a D9 earth mover. And they cleared it off.

We looked at it and said, "If it rains, it will be a mud pit because it's winter."

So, I called a friend of mine in Kailua, Mike Kincaid, and said, "Hey, Mike, do you know where I can get some gravel or crushed coral?"

"What for?"

I explained about the parking lot, and Mike called Duane Steel, who owns Grace Pacific, The next morning, there were three, giant semis that were filled with crushed coral with another piece of equipment to flatten and grade the lot. It was a miracle.

We also were trying to figure out how to get people around because you can only get so many people into Mākaha. So, a friend of mine, Buddy Reed who lived in Honolulu at the time and knew some people, sent out one of those shuttles that run around Waikīkī. And the funny thing was that we didn't actually "shuttle" a lot of people. But, Luana Keaulana decided to be the conductor of the trolley, and all those kids must have ridden the trolley a hundred times. It was like a Disneyland ride for those kids.

Rell the Instigator) Sonja Evensen & Marilyn Link

SONJA: She had that multiplicity. She wasn't only a local Mākaha girl. She was the one who talked me into hula, by the way. She talked me into everything. She goes, "You've got the best *kumu hula* right down the street. Why don't you do that?"

And I go, "I'm *haole*; I can't do that."

And she goes, "Why not?" So, she talked me into that, and I ended up loving it.

She just had friends from all over. Every time [I went over to her house], I'd meet somebody. She had all kinds of people at her house at any given time. And they were all different. I don't even know who her friends were. She just met all kinds of people and made friends like that, and took them in, and took every opportunity. I don't think you had to be a surfer to be her friend. You had to be interesting. She was interested in everything.

MARILYN: That's what brought us together. I met Sonja through Rell. I was there the first time she was on a sailboard. We have less in common than Rell and I did because I'm not even living next door to Sonja like I was with Rell. There are several friends I'm still close with because of Rell. Like you said, she was the instigator. She was the glue—the original field marshal. She was the one who organized and orchestrated. She was incredibly resourceful. She would put people together.

SONJA: Oh god, she was a matchmaker for me. But that was a disaster. She had a really funny taste in men, at least for me.

MARILYN: She didn't really think about it, and, then, afterward you'd go, "What were you thinking?" And she'd laugh about it.

She had different levels of consciousness, too. Like, if you were at her house, she was never focused on just one thing. She'd be sitting at her dining room table, looking at the newspaper, her yellow pad was always there, the phone would ring, and someone would walk in the door. There would be all this distraction, and she dealt with it. But, you were never sure when she was setting you up with someone just how distracted she was at the time. It was sometimes, "Hello, maybe you meant to set me up with the person on the phone but you set me up with the guy who walked through the door.

SONJA: All these little projects…she was such a good project person. That's why it was good she never worked in a regular job like a bank. She just pieced together pieces of work, and it all worked out. She played her own game by her own rules, and it was so refreshing.

A Sharp Eye; An Eloquent Tongue ⟩ Sonja Evensen

JUST LISTENING TO her commentary, it was so funny. I remember this one trip where we went to Kaua'i with 'Ilima Kalama and Lance Ho'okano for a contest at Pine Trees in Hanalei, and she dragged us through every single antique shop. I was so sick of it, but the commentary was great because she didn't miss one single little moment of seeing something and pointing it out. And the way she'd point it out, you'd go, "Oh, wow."

That whole thing we called a "Rellism." To me, it signifies the way Rell sees things because nobody saw things the way Rell saw them. Even to this day, I say in my head, "What would Rell say about this?"

The Long, Hard Paddle ⟩ Jim Kempton

RELL ARRANGED THIS whole excursion to French Polynesia because she wanted to go to Tahiti to learn the Tahitian hula, which she thought was more authentic and less commercialized than the hula in Hawai'i at the time. She went to a number of hula *hālau* in Tahiti on this trip, and, later, she and Jeff Divine and I met up with Rabbit Bartholomew and several other pro surfers who were on Tahiti to do a photo shoot.

It was when we were first were discovering the outer islands like Huahine. The ship voyage was one of the greatest experiences of our lives. We took a freighter from Papeete over to Fare [Fare Suisse]. It's one of those things that all the local people use as the highway. You can fly. There are airports there. But, the local people don't really have the money to do that. So, when they want to go visit their relatives, they book a passage on the freighters that carry all the goods to the outer islands. You get on in the late afternoon and go across the channel at night.

So, all these incredible Tahitian people get aboard, and they bring their cages with their chickens in them, and all their stuff is wrapped in their *pareos* tied to a stick like the railroad hobos did in the old days on the mainland. And they lay their mats down and undo all those bundles and spread them out with fruit and dried meat and fish, and they party. Everyone joins in, playing 'ukuleles and singing and dancing hula until they fall asleep. And you wake up coming into the beautiful harbor in Fare on Huahine.

I don't know if it's still the case because I haven't been back there in so long. But, the way you got out to the waves was you tied your board to a two-man canoe, and you paddled your canoe out to the reef and tied your canoe to the reef. You, then, walked along the shallow reef with your *zories*, and, when you got to the pass, you stuck your sandals on these reed sticks so they wouldn't wash away. Then, you hopped off the reef into the pass with your board.

This wasn't the main pass at Fare, where the boats go through the big channel. It was the one far down to the left of that. There's a good little left there, but it has that staghorn coral that and comes up in these long, rough horns. The surf was not really big, which was worse because the smaller waves break right on the shallowest coral. It's a hollow, top-to-bottom wave where you have to pull in the barrel or just get past the reef.

I caught a wave and got pitched straight down, feet first. And the staghorn coral came up my leg like someone took a paring knife and skinned an apple. There were these ribbons of flesh that looked just like pasta, a quarter of an inch wide and sixteen inches long hanging from just below mid-thigh almost to my ankle. Just looking at these ribbons was enough to make your head spin.

I couldn't just yank them off. You needed a knife or scissors to cut them off. The blood was oozing and wouldn't stop, and we had already been told to watch out for the sharks. They won't ever bother you because they're well-fed, but, now, they're smelling blood. So, I got up on the reef, and I'm looking at these things dangling off my leg, and, of course, everyone else is off surfing.

Then, Rell paddles over and asks, "Do you want to paddle in?" By this time, I can't even look at the lacerations without getting dizzy. So, she says, "Okay, I'll paddle in with you."

So, we tie our boards to the back of a canoe, and we jump into what was very primitive—just a dugout. Of course, Rell is a canoe paddler, and I'm not paddler. I'm in the back, and I can see all these muscles in her back. She's stroking, and we're several hundred yards offshore. So, it's a serious paddle. It's super hot. The midday sun is beating down. My head is reeling, and I'm looking in the bottom of the canoe, and the water is turning from pink to red.

Rell is paddling me in to shore and chanting, "Paddle, Jim, paddle, paddle."

And I'm thinking, "I'm glad you're here." Anything could have happened. I could have passed out. I could have been chumming for sharks.

The waves were really good, and nobody wanted to stop. I couldn't have made it to shore on my own. That was Rell. Everybody is having a good session and you might have gotten in by yourself, but Rell is the kind of person who climbs into the canoe and paddles in with you. And everybody else is like, "Bummahs, brah. One less guy in the lineup."

Here were all these guys that we were surfing with, and it's Rell who paddled me in and took me to a clinic to get my wounds treated.

Insight from a Goddess ⟩ Merideth Moncata

THERE ARE SO many Rell stories…every conversation…every note written. She was great with the handmade, from-the-heart, from-the-sea *mahalo*, as well as the little ant people that she would draw on the contest applications. I still draw them to this day. They were always a celebration of "woohoo" to life. The most important story for me is the birth of the LG and the WG. It changed the way I see my life and my world and myself. And it always reminds me that she was my friend.

It began with a conversation. We were joking around about being spectacular, special people… that we could do anything we wanted…but that we would need supernatural powers in order to maintain our "specialness." So, Rell decided that, on this island, I would be the Windward Goddess and she would be the Leeward Goddess. It was a joke, but I would send off notes to her, "LG," and I would sign off by writing "the all-loving but powerless WG."

Having the Queen of Mākaha, someone as spectacular as Rell, to think I was this special person and now, it seemed, a "goddess" sort of made me think. "What are the responsibilities of being a goddess?" Celebrate for any reason; have a selfless attitude; always say something nice to someone else; have an open mind; inspire others; and really just to "live *aloha*" just like Rell did…I mean how she really lived. When somebody asks my preference about what I want to be…maybe the first lady or the queen bee…I say, "Actually, I prefer a goddess," and it brings Rell right back into my heart. Now, I tell people all the time that I'm a goddess.

Savoring Every Moment ⟩ Caroline Zimmerman

LIFE IS, INDEED, quite strange, miraculous, and never predictable. A huge gift in my life was the time I spent at Mākaha with Rell as a guest in her home, her Mākaha, her waves and her "family." Rell left me with an incredible sense of living life, *la dolce vita*, to put it in Italian terms, and how to squeeze the juice out of every moment and savor it to the last drop.

I was diagnosed with breast cancer just as Rell began her decline. I was faced with the same destiny. It broke her heart to see it happen to me, as with her other friends. She witnessed, one by one. Yet, she was always up front about her experience and advised me to be aggressive in the fight and seek out the best possible treatment.

The last time I saw Rell, we both were bald, feeling pretty frumpy together. But, we still managed to get into town to indulge in some "cocoa puffs" at the bakery and go to her favorite Thai restaurant.

I do have numerous stories to tell. But, my words are awkward and inadequate. I've done best, I believe, with expressing my emotions in paint. Take a look at the "seven seas" gallery on my website crowzone.com. There, you'll find a painting of her home.

The day I received the news that Rell had died, I was in my studio trying to work. It was the nadir of my life, as I had already lost so much to my illness and lost my marriage. Painting was all I had to keep me afloat. My friend Malinda Chouinard phoned me and told me. I collapsed in a heap, and felt so alone and abandoned…like one of Rell's little, glass balls drifting in the sea. Then, in an instant, something came over me…like a wave… and I felt an awakening. I heard her voice and felt her love of life around me. The little, glass ball had found a new shore. I knew what to do…to paint an homage to her… to her 'ohana and to all the treasured memories.

I decided to paint her home from photos I had taken over the years. And what a bittersweet journey that was. Each detail brought back a flood of memories…the sound of her music, her voice as she would do dishes in the kitchen, Shaney-boy lounging on the *lanai*, the cooing of doves and caress of tradewinds, smells of plumeria in the trees…. I was there again. I brought these memories to life. The painting I titled "Little Hula Heaven."

"Little Hula Heaven" painted by Caroline Zimmerman

Mentor & Guide

Under Rell's Spell ⟩ Robyn Eastman

THAT WAS THE whole thing about "Life with Rell." It was about relationships from the very beginning.

It was my first summer in California and my first year really away from my kids. Tom and I decided, since Tom didn't have to work, we would try to keep the kids stabilized through our divorce, and he would live in the house with the kids because I would have to work.

So, I made my way into the work world using all I had—my writing abilities and, others say, a nice personality, and a black belt in the martial arts. I was well armed, or so I thought.

California and its entrepreneurial atmosphere brought projects to my door. One that intrigued me the most was the surfing world. They were a strange bunch of people—professional doctors, lawyers, and dentists to what they called the "beachboys"—all in the midst of putting a surf circuit together for some of the watermen I'd met. This group of people used Hawaiian words and had stories and music that entranced me. Little did I know the power it would really have over me.

It was a different world than I had known in the cold winters outside Chicago.

We were all in preparation for the Oceanside Surf Club's annual contest. As the contest neared, people in the club began talking more and more about this Hawaiian woman who was coming for the contest. She was the greatest woman surfer in the world. She actually had won contests all over the world. They said her name was Rell. I loved the name and somehow knew the woman who went with it had to be something special.

In the midst of all this, I had fallen in love with a married man, another legend surfer. (Mind you, his wife called me in the middle of it and said not to worry.) Whispers ran rampant behind our backs, but we didn't care. It was mad, crazy, passionate love that erases the rest of the world. 'Ilima raved about Rell, too. Not only was she one of the top women surfers in the world, but she was also a woman of great magic.

I was on the outskirts looking in toward a group of people who had grown up together and who had tons of stories with each other. They had a history that, at that point, was hard to describe. It was addictive, though. I was enthralled working at the sign-in table, smelling the salt on bodies, hearing the crashing of the waves, feeling the level of excitement the competition was mustering.

All of a sudden, as if out of thin air, this bubbly, Hawaiian sprite of a woman came running up with her board.

"Hi, I'm Rell. Can you watch my board a minute? I'll be right back!" She bounded off before I could even answer. That was Rell. Everyone took care of her. She knew it and lived it. What's more, everyone loved taking care of her…from raking her yard to carrying her board to holding her shopping bags when we went shopping.

Off she went, smiling hello to most everyone along her way. The only other smile I thought was that special was my godmother's. ([Rell] was like my mother, and our relationship was the most rooted in my soul.) This new woman had an energy about her like I'd known her forever. It always felt like that from that day forward. Over the weekend, we had meals and conversations, as I simply got to hang with Rell.

She was my friend, my sister, my mentor, and the one who taught me the meaning of *aloha*.

My education began at the contest as she explained different kinds of waves and conditions. She whispered the background of each surfer we would meet…what they were well known for, who hung out with whom. She was my own personal "Who's Who" book on the world of surfing.

Though I had felt a bit ostracized within the surf community, Rell spent much of the weekend with 'Ilima and I and heard of our plans to move to the islands. She made me promise to call her as soon as we got there. She knew what my new life was going to be. Being with a real beachboy is a wild ride. They love the wave more than themselves.

We moved over a few months later. I moved to Hawai'i sight unseen, with no job and no friends except for Rell. I called her the day we arrived. She came over the next day and picked us up in her old, yellow, beach cruiser station wagon. She sent 'Ilima off to the beach, and I entered the Widemann Street house for the first time.

Rell always joked that it was held together by termites. The rickety beach house was almost like a part of the family. Rell had it stuffed with Hawaiian antiques. There was not a place that wasn't stuffed with something. The garage had stacks of racks with surfboards of every shape and size. More surfboards, broken and worn, were strewn in piles in various places around the yard. There was fishing gear and nets and Hawaiian slings (like sling shots to catch fish). Chairs of all sizes and shapes were everywhere because, more often than not, they were filled with the people who had paraded through all year long.

A plumeria tree sat in one corner. I soon learned that plumeria *lei* were Rell's favorite, and the tree offered up its bounty for many a *lei*. The *lei* represented the circle of life that surrounded Rell. There was a circle of people who brought a part of themselves to Rell's door—each one of them representing a flower. My life began to fill with the delicious stories of Hawaiian Days. Rell, from our first meeting, opened her heart to me and allowed me to learn what "*aloha*" really means.

I moved to Hanalei with a pipe dream of 'Ilima having a fishing boat. He would take me with him while he fished and I wrote. I had been a dreamer from small-kid times and knew how to make stories that sounded much better than real life.

The reality of paying bills and day-to-day living arrived. I slowly widened my network of people (with lots of help from Rell). I picked up any job I could get and, at one point, even

cleaned houses. I had to learn that no righteous surfer would be working if the waves were up. I was now in "life is lived by the wave" world. Everyone was like water gypsies, and Rell was very much the same.

We moved to Maui by the second week. By the next month, Rell told me to "come by her" for a week or so…back to O'ahu. This was my initiation into how my life would look for the next ten years.

Rell said my first lesson is to know, remember, and "nevah, nevah" forget.

It's customary when you go to someone's house on another island that you bring a special delicacy from your island. Each island has items that are filled with memories. And usually they were sweet. Although Maui was known for the Azeka ribs, Rell was always more interested in Komoda Bakery cream puffs and donuts on a stick. A box of each was usually enough. But, if it were a holiday, you had to bring more.

I dutifully made sure I had time to go to the bakery before I caught the plane to O'ahu.

"Remember, if you don't have those white boxes in your hand, I won't pick you up." She'd let out her full-bodied laugh that ensured she was kidding. But, then, she would add with mischievous eyes, "Eh, I'm *keeding*." I was naïve, so I never took a chance and made sure I always had the white boxes.

Mind you, she always did the same. When I'd pick her up on Maui, she brought *liliko'i* rainbow cakes and *poi*.

Our days at Rell's always begun very early in the morning. Wave patrol. First stop, Wai'anae Circle K for coffee with flavored creams and a glazed pastry with a chocolate dollop on the top. Then, it was straight to Mākaha Beach, tooling down the one lane highway with multicolor surfboards hanging out the back. Readiness was a rule of beach life.

Rell couldn't go in, though, until she did the surf report. She was in radio and covered the big canoe races as well as the surf contests. And, every morning, she would collect the news from her reliable sources at each beach and put together a surf report that was crisp and alive and funny and incorporated the people. She always told stories, and she'd put someone's name in that she knew would be listening. When it was you, you felt special all day. Everyone needs acknowledgment, and Rell acknowledged those around her with humor and with admiration for their good qualities so that it gave everyone a sense of belonging. Ultimately, in all our times together, it was never "my family" and "your family." We were all one big family.

In radio, Rell painted a picture of each beach and the people. She even had the creatures of the sea come alive in anecdotes and stories. Listening to her gave me my first broadcasting lessons, though I didn't know at the time that I would be in radio, too.

Once the report was done, everyone grabbed a surfboard, bodyboard, flippers, diving masks, Hawaiian slings, and *rubbah slippahs*, and off we went for the first dip of the day—fully prepared for an "anything can happen day."

Not having grown up on the beach, I usually waited for the afternoon session. It was chilly, and my enjoyment came from watching the addiction get quenched. Once you've lived in the circles of surfers, you learn that "no waves" is like a session of PMS on steroids. Moods rose and fell with the size of the waves.

This particular week, though, was my "Mākaha 101." And it was the time I first learned about Rell's cancer.

Each day, Rell would teach me another morsel—the names of waves, the face, the curl, shortboards versus longboards, hang ten, and what constitutes a good ride and a bad one. But very, very most important was "beach etiquette." Rell's house was several blocks from Mākaha. Mākaha was well known for being owned by its neighbors. If you were a stranger (especially one with white skin), you'd better be there as a friend of a regular. Rell made sure I was watched out for from the start. It wasn't until the surf contests, though, that I remembered names and the wide variety of personalities that lined the shore every day.

Rell was only a few years younger than I, and, at those ages, doing all the activities we did, you don't think about diseases or think that anything can debilitate you. Rell never spoke about the cancer in a negative way. It was the same as the huge waves she faced—it was something you dive into and ride. It was actually Homer Barrett, who stayed on the beach with me, who told me. He and his wife Eileen were an older couple, close friends of Buffalo and his wife Momi. In the hierarchy of Mākaha, they were the "final word." Though Rell was called the queen of Mākaha, they were in the "emperor" range. Disagreements, issues, and problems were brought to Buff and Momi. They straightened them out. This beach was a huge family, and, no matter how much fighting might go on, when the going got tough, everyone stuck together.

Especially during the morning sessions, Homer and I would sit at the picnic table in the corner of the beach, and he would tell me the stories of all the players. He told me of Rell's beginning bouts with cancer, the chemo, the relationship with her then-husband, Frank, how hard it had been. Men often don't handle disease of a loved one well. He dealt with his anger and sadness by making jokes.

My role quickly emerged. I was Rell's buffer. She didn't have to deal with something when I was there. We spent our days and nights learning about Hanalei and Hawaiians and doing arts and crafts that honored the ocean and its bounty. Rell became the first really close girlfriend I'd ever had. For some women it's different. But, I know, for me, I had not had women friends. My time with Rell opened me to the world of circles of women.

The constant flow of people included many women who became a part of our particular circle. In this circle, we counseled each other through our relationships with me…with the world. But, mostly, it opened up our relationships with ourselves. We were all in our late thirties and early forties. These times were a reckoning. As Rell faced each moment with her cancer fight, we walked the moments with her. When someone brought her a homeopathic idea for a new cure, we all took the cure with her. From mushrooms to *noni*, we took as much of all the same natural medicines as we could to support her.

Rell was a singularly beautiful woman. As with most Hawaiian women, she had long, brown hair that floated around her like a mermaid when she dove for red *kūmū*. At one point in her chemo, she lost all of her hair. It was devastating for her, though she didn't let on to most people that it was. She still went to the

surf each day and would wear a baseball cap surfing to protect her from the sun and from the embarrassment.

One weekend, it was a contest day at Mākaha. From early morning, there was a special sparkle in the air. People would sleep in tents all along the shore. We'd still go for the early peek of the waves and greet everyone as we walked by their sizzling grills filled with fresh fish caught for breakfast. Everyone gave morsels to us, and there were always the warm, sleepy-eyed good mornings.

This day, we went back to Rell's house to pack for a day at the beach. Rell put on her hat, and we stuffed ourselves in the yellow tuna station wagon with coolers, beach chairs, extra towels, Hawaiian slings, and every other just-in-case item you could think of.

When we arrived, the water was filled with the gang testing the early morning waves while the judges were setting up their stands and tables. As we looked out squinting through the diamond sparkles that spread across the early morning water, we noticed something strange. Rell walked out onto the beach, and the guys began walking out of the water. They surrounded Rell with big grins on their faces and all wearing baseball caps. As she looked around, each surfer grabbed the hat off his head, and Rell found herself in the middle of a sea of bald heads matching hers. We all laughed and cried at the same time.

This was Mākaha—tough *blahlahs* who would fight about dumb stuff at the drop of a hat, but who would whip off their own silly, pink and white hats to reveal their freshly shaved heads in honor of their queen.

A Fine Eye for Design ⟩ John Moore

WHEN SHE AND Dave Parmenter got married, he used to come over to Raging Isle to get boards glassed. So, while he was over there doing all that, Rell would hang out at Patagonia and over at my store Strong Current.

I had that whole LeRoy Grannis wall with all the Grannis historical photographs. And every single picture Rell could tell you a story about.

She said to me, "Hey, you should make a T-shirt with a hula girl here instead of a surfer guy."

So, we went through this whole thing about how this is "kind of our logo" and "nah, nah, nah."

Then, she said, "If I draw one, will you do it?"

I said, "Yeah. Sure."

So, she drew it, and we've still got it. Her shirt has a band of bamboo and a hula girl, and we still use it. That's what I wore to her funeral at Mākaha.

Straight to the Top
~ Bonga Perkins

THERE WAS THIS event at Mākaha, and all the top surfers in the world came over here to do it—obviously a lot of money and prestige for this one event.

Throughout the day, Rell was telling me, "Man, keep surfing the way you're surfing and this thing is yours. Sew it up." And that motivated me to go out there because, coming from her, the queen of Mākaha… somebody like that telling me something really good at that point was something I really needed to hear. It was a boost of confidence.

So, I made it to the finals, and I was happy about that. It was a forty-minute final, and I thought I did really well. There were four to six foot waves—real performance surf. There were a lot of waves—an even playing field. So, the only person who would to take you out would be yourself.

The finals came up. I was doing really well, and, when I paddled in, I felt good. I was in the lead. When they read the results, I came up a half a point shy. To top the whole story off, Rell came up to me and said, "Hey, look. In my eyes, you won. I know it's not maybe what you want to hear, but you're the best surfer in the world."

She inspired a lot of people by giving constructive criticism and words of encouragement. When you're going through these heats and you hear people telling you good luck, that you're doing well, it makes all the difference. Her voice is so appealing that it sinks in. So, when she tells you something, it's motivating and inspiring.

The next year, I won the world championship.

Guidance and Generosity ⟩ Sunny Garcia

I USED TO get up on the weekends early in the morning and walk from Māʻili Point to Mākaha. Rell used to have a bunch of boards from Local Motion that she let all the kids who didn't have boards use. So, I'd get up early and walk to Mākaha when I knew there would be waves. You know, first come, first served. I'd be there earlier than everybody else and borrow whatever board she would lend me.

There are a lot things that people don't know that she did for everybody. Everybody knows she was generous, but they didn't know how generous she was and how far out of the way she would go for the unfortunate kids down there. She helped me quite a bit. I was fortunate that I had people like Bird Mahelona and Rell and the whole Keaulana family to help me. The surfing part was easy for me. The guidance part was where I really needed some help.

A Menehune Trick ⟩ Sunny Garcia

I DON'T THINK I talked to Auntie Rell for a while after she told me I couldn't compete in the Menehune Contest because I was winning so much. For me, that was my favorite event. It was the first event I won when I was eleven, and I was just pissed. She said I couldn't surf in it because she wanted Sam to win. Fortunately for Sam, he ended up winning. But, unfortunately for me, I didn't get to surf my last year in my favorite event.

It was a big deal because that was all there was on the Wai'anae Coast—the Menehune Contest. Rell's contest always had good prizes and stuff, and, even though I won the thing every year, I didn't have the sponsors. So, it was nice to get a new board and all the prizes that came along with it. I didn't get one that year, so I was pissed.

But that's all right. Rell was always looking out for the rest of the kids. She couldn't have her nephew win every single year. Rell was always good to the kids, and that was her main concern. It didn't matter whether you were related to her or not. She treated everybody the same, and that's why everybody loved her.

Sea School's in Session
Brickwood Galuteria

WHEN WE BOTH worked at KCCN radio, Rell used to give the surf report.

Whenever the surf was good, she would say, "Surf's up. No need go to school today."

And I'd say, "Rell, what you doing? No tell the kids no need go to school today because the surf is good."

And she'd say, "Well, there's lessons out there in the waves, too."

"Aaaah, you banana, you."

Kau Kau for da Keiki ⟩ Glen Moncata

RELL'S BIG THING at the Menehune Contest was the fact that these kids come down to the beach, and the parents don't feed them. They're always starving, and they always want a drink. So, when we first started, we would get Pizza Hut to give us some pizza and stuff like that. It was always a hassle because you always had to beg and borrow. So, one year, Rell goes, "Let's just barbecue."

"Oh, god. Here we go again." And this has turned into a real legacy for kids contests now because we went out there, and everybody brought their Webers down, and the guys always cook. We cooked hamburgers and hot dogs for all the kids on the beach.

What this has now turned into is I have a twenty-one-foot, mobile kitchen that I tow behind my car and take to all the surf contests and cook for all the kids. It's because of that contest that you go to a contest now (it doesn't matter if it's a Quiksilver contest or anything) but it's kind of expected that you feed the kids. That's another legacy that Rell brought to the surf contests.

The funny thing is that you never know how many people you're going to feed. So, at the last contest, we served three-hundred-and-eighty plates of spaghetti on the beach at Mākaha. That's not only the kids. The parents are standing there eating, too. It's quite the scene. And, every time there's food left over or we buy too much, we go, "Hey, we're at Mākaha. This food will be gone." You serve lunch at twelve, and you've got three pans of chili and rice still there, enough to feed another ten people. By four o'clock, there's nothing left. After they've surfed, the kids come up and go, "You got anything to eat?"

I think that was Rell's thing, too. She cared so much for the kids. She would tell me, "It doesn't matter how much money you spend on that. Just get enough for the kids."

Another Expensive Inspiration 〉 Glen Moncata

RELL WOULD ALWAYS call me with great ideas, and they would always cost me money. But, most of the things that she did, that she would be adamant about me helping her with, always came out perfect. She had a real knack for looking into different projects and having me put them together.

The first one was the coloring books. She called me up one day and said, "I've got to talk to you about something."

I said, "Okay. Come on over. What is it going to cost me this time?"

So, she drove to Kailua from Mākaha. She had a pad with her, and, on that pad, she had *'ukulele* songs. She said, "Wouldn't it be great to put an *'ukulele* coloring book together so kids could to learn to play the *'ukulele* and color in the book?"

"It sounds great. But, I don't know what it's going to cost and who will do the illustrations."

"Don't worry about the illustrations, I'll get those done. You just figure out how to pay for the books."

And, in the three or four years that we did the coloring books, it was the most successful thing at the Menehune Contest. One was the 'ukulele book, and another was the stories of the little boy who was surfing in the Menehune Contest. If anybody has one of those right now, they are treasures. They were one of the best things in the goodie bags. When you passed them out to the kids, they didn't know what they were. But, then, they started looking at them, and you'd see kids with 'ukulele trying to play the songs because they had the charts to show you where to put your fingers.

Sharing and Caring 〉 Desiree DeSoto

I WAS SURFING in town a lot. I just got back from college. You know, you're young…you don't know the etiquette…it's all about you. You're not thinking about anyone else in the water; you just want to catch that next good wave. And I had the swimming skills. I was four-time all-American. So, I could catch any wave I wanted, and I usually did.

At Mākaha, I could get away with that. I just had tunnel vision. I really was close-minded. I can see how my brain has developed to see everybody now instead of just what I wanted to see.

I would go to town and catch every wave I wanted, and I guess I was pissing off everyone at Ala Moana Bowls. It's pretty intense; it's like the Pipeline of the summertime.

It got back to Auntie Rell through Jeannie Chesser that "Desiree was coming out with a bunch of girls, and they were catching all the waves, and they weren't respecting the lineup and the old-timers."

I came down to the beach at Mākaha one day, and she brought it up cordially. "So, you been surfing in town, eh?"

I'm like, "Yeah, we've been going to Ala Moana. I love that wave."

She's like, "Well, Dez, it's cool. It's a great wave, but just follow this direction. For every one wave you catch, you've got to let three go by."

I'm like, "Three nice ones or three swells?"

"No, three nice ones. You got to share."

It helped me because I respected her, and she helped me to see things. I don't think anybody at that time of my life could have come up to me and directed me. You had to be somebody special for me to listen. I had that kind of attitude, "Who are *you*? I'm not going to listen to *you*."

I thought I was invincible. But, because it came from Auntie Rell, I took it in and saw where she was coming from. It opened my mind a lot going into the water. I thought more about sharing instead of just myself.

Auntie Rell gave me my first surfboard. I was eight or nine, and I was only using my dad's surfboard, bodyboards, things like that. And I just, basically, started surfing on my bodyboard.

Auntie Rell came up to me one day and handed me a Local Motion *fish*. It was beautiful, and I loved it. I mean, that was my first surfboard. Auntie Pua gave me my first bikini. I valued both of them more than most things in my life.

The Gift of Giving Back ⟩ Luana Froiseth

RELL WAS ON a mission, and her mission was really surfing. The more she surfed and the more she met people, the more she wanted to spread Hawai'i throughout the world… the "*aloha* spirit" more than anything else.

I think when she got cancer she wanted to spread that even more. Her philosophy of life, that competition, it was still there ninety-nine percent. But, that other one percent was that she wanted, however much more life she had on earth, to spend as much time as she could with everybody she knew and just give everything she could for the rest of the life she had left to her.

Passing On ⟩ Luana Froiseth

EVERYBODY WHO WENT out to her house in Mākaha, she would encourage by saying, "Stay over. Stay over. We can go surfing in the morning and do dawn patrol." Friends liked to stay there because there was so much love in that home. It was so Hawaiian. It had everything in there that made you feel at home. The dinners were good. The company was good. All you did was laugh inside that house. That's why everybody liked to go out there, even when the surf wasn't up.

It was just to go hang out and talk story, surf all day long, come back, talk story again, meet new people over there. A lot of people went over there at any old time of the day and said,

"Howzit, Rell?" People came from all over the world. I met a lot of people over there who I would never have met any other place except at Rell's Motel.

Why would people come over there except for the surf? When the surf wasn't there, you just sit down and talk story, or, "Come on. Let's go diving. Or let's go swimming or hiking or do something else." It was like a vacation home away from home. You were so comfortable there, whether you were in the house or outside the house. You could do anything you wanted to, and you never had to bring your board because Rell had millions of boards that anyone could borrow. Even if Rell wasn't home, you could come over there, take a board, go surf, and bring it back. She trusted you. It was amazing because her boards weren't locked down. It was pretty sweet.

Rell left two boards at my house for when she would come into town and she wanted to go surf.

As she started to get more and more sick, I asked her, "What do you want me to do with the boards? You want me to take them back to your house?"

She said, "No, just keep them. The boards are for you." I actually scored on those two boards because one was a Donald Takayama and the other was a board she won.

Everybody who comes over wants to surf says, "Can I borrow a board?"

And we say, "Yep, you can borrow it, one of these two. Pick one. These are our 'ohana boards. They came from Rell, and we are passing it on."

Scalded and Scolded ⟩ Fletcher Chouinard

I WENT TO Tahiti with my parents, my sister, Rell, Sam George, and Caroline…to Tahiti, Moorea, and Huahine…and we got a lot of good surf. But, Rell was pretty sick through a lot of it. So, she couldn't get in the water as much as she wanted.

She gave me the most intense lecture of my life there. My mom was freaking out at me about something and just being irrational pissed off. So, I snapped at her and said, "Stop bitching at me."

Rell overheard it, and just laid into me, "She's your mom, and it doesn't matter if she's being irrational. You never speak to your mother like that."

It was pretty intense. I've certainly always tried to treat my mom with more respect since then. I don't even think I realized I was being that disrespectful or that I made that big of an impact on anybody when I talked up until that point. It was the way Rell was able to make me feel like I was letting her and everybody down when I was an asshole. I felt awful about it afterward.

Other than that, it was a really fun trip. Rell spent a lot of time taking pictures of everybody and watching. It was also a cool time because Buffalo and a whole bunch of people were there, too, renting a house on Moorea, and we got to crash their whole party.

Serious Scoldings ∤ Kimo Kauihou

THE WAY I like to surf Mākaha is probably like most surfers. I like a lot of speed. I like to go way out on the shoulder and then cut back into the curl and whitewash. It's still how I surf. One day, we were surfing out there, and it was a pretty fun size, three to five feet. I was surfing like I normally surf, and Rell was surfing, too. I was on a wave, and it was a little blinding because the sun comes over the mountain in the morning and shines in your eyes. I had gone way out on the shoulder of the wave, and Rell was paddling out on the shoulder, and we barely missed running into each other. Rell turned around and said words that I don't dare repeat. She just scolded me right there. I still surf like that, but getting *cracks* from her was pretty humbling. She always put me in my place and let me know the hierarchy and the rules out there in the waves.

I guess I remember all the scoldings because, all the other times, Rell was always cool and mellow. Whenever she got mad at me, she was [only] mad at the time. But, then, everything was good after that. Even in the scoldings, she was the queen that she was. That was how she held herself up. She cared enough not to just look the other way. I felt kind of privileged. I don't know if everyone else got scoldings, too, but I was always getting counseled or scolded by her.

One day, my compressor was down. So, Dave Parmenter told me, "Come over to my house, and paint your boards over here."

I was airbrushing my board, and Dave and Rell were kind of watching me because nobody really goes on their property and in their home and works. They were just checking me out.

Then, when I'm done painting my board, I go and rinse the paint out in the drain, and Rell had one fit.

"Do you know where that drain leads to? It leads straight to the ocean. Don't throw your stuff down there. All the drains and pipes lead to the ocean."

That was a first time I had really thought about that. So, I got corrected again.

I knew Rell since we moved here in '87. She was always good to my family and me…always had a lot of *aloha* for us. And she managed to share a little of it with everybody, gracefully and smoothly.

Auntie to All the Keiki ⟩ Kalani Robb

ONE OF THE neatest things about Auntie Rell was that, obviously, she was an older lady and we were young kids. But, there's something about the way that she was always like a kid. She always knew how we were feeling, and she always knew personalities. The instant you'd meet her, she would know what kind of kid you were and what she could do to help you out. She always knew what she could do to make you a better surfer or maybe change your attitude if you're a little punk.

She was always good at being able to see what a kid's like and send you out to the surf or somehow direct you somewhere else instead saying, "Hey, kids. Shut up, already. Go in the surf. You two surf a little longer and get rid of your energy and calm down a little bit."

She was basically like a school, teaching you how to do things and teaching you good morals. She was one of those surf ladies where you go, "Okay, she's not my real auntie." But, you'd want her to be your auntie because she was so cool. She was an auntie for so many people.

I never surfed Mākaha before surfing in Rell's Menehune Contest. That event started me off surfing Mākaha and the West Side and meeting people and getting used to a new side of the island. When you're young, it's like you've never been here. The West Side is so rugged, and you go, "How could this nice lady be from this side?"

She was like one of those ladies who a lot of surfing girls should be aspiring to be like because she wasn't a just a surfer. She was a goodwill ambassador when she went somewhere. People would be, "Whoa! Rell Sunn! That's the real Hawaiian style. She's got that positive *aloha* spirit." The Hawaiians have a rep for being tough, not always the *aloha* spirit, more like "Don't cut him off or he'll beat you up," or "Don't do this or don't do that." They're so gnarly.

But, Rell was like a Duke Kahanamoku, where she was just positive— nothing negative.

She set a really good example for everybody.

She was someone you always aspired to be like when you got older, whether you're a girl or a boy. She set a precedent for how to treat kids in Hawai'i.

Appearances are Deceiving ⟩ Randy Rarick

IN THE MID 1960S, I used to surf the Mākaha International contest, and I was better friends with Martha. There was Martha, Anela, and Rell, and Rell was kind of not as good a surfer as her sisters in the early days. She got stuck with her boyfriend or husband early on, so she wasn't out there surfing like the other two were.

Then, when shortboards started coming in, her sisters sort of backed off. Rell stayed on the West Side, while the family moved to Maui.

She kind of came into her own on shortboards because she wasn't very good on longboards. She was better suited to ride a shortboard. When we started the pro tour in the mid 1970s, she was one of the prime women competitors. Rell went on the world tour, but she wasn't a very good competitive surfer. She was too graceful and too smooth. It was a really nice trait to watch, very pleasing. But, in terms of what you had to do competitively, she always came up just short because she never had that extra little bit of panache you need to win the tournament.

That was good because she had such a pleasing style that was nice to watch in a free-surf kind of situation. So, she was involved in the mid 1970s into the 1980s on the women's world tour. In the late 1980s, we had a women's event in Hale'iwa, one of the pro events, and the sponsor had provided all this gear, bathing suits, women's tops, and this and that.

Back then, the setup was much smaller than it is now. The judges would sit on a three-section scaffolding. You could throw the thing up in an hour with a canvas wraparound. And I'll never forget Rell. She came in from behind and lifted the canvas thing up where all the free stuff was, and she *cockaroached* all this stuff. I was thinking, "What are you doing ripping all this stuff off?" I was so bummed. But, it turned out she was taking all this gear to give to all the underprivileged kids over on the West Side.

Spreading the Surf Stoke ⟩ Donald Takayama

I KNEW RELL when she was just a little kid. She and her sister Martha and I used to compete in the Mākaha International contest. She was just a terrific, local surfer. I wasn't surprised by how good Rell and Martha were because I used to go to Mākaha and saw these little girls out there surfing every day. I'd go down there and talk to them, and they were kind of shy. I was fourteen and they were nine and ten, and I'd say, "Hey you're pretty good, eh? Showoffs." But, it was really neat.

As surfing grew, so did Rell's heart—her *aloha* with the love of Hawai'i with every generation to keep them off the streets. Through the love of surfing she felt the *aloha spirit* of surfing. What really got her excited in the sport of surfing was that she wanted to share it all with the kids. Keep them surfing keeps them happy…gives them something to look forward to.

Through surfing, you get one good wave and it really makes your day. To paddle out and get two good waves totally makes your day. To have an ultimate day, you get four or five excellent waves. It never stops. You just want to get into it more and more. The competitive side is really great. The kids go out and practice, and they just want to get better and better and look forward to something. She just tried to share all that she had with all the kids.

I had talked to her when she had a year left. I said, "Rell, how are you doing?"

And she said, "I'm doing okay."

I said, "Rell, don't bullshit me. How are you really doing?"

And she responded, "I only have a year because of the cancer."

So, I said, "What do you want? What do you really want?"

And she replied, "I need some time. I want to do this Menehune [Contest] thing for the kids. If I can only get five to eight more years…. I have all these plans, but I feel like I'm being cut short."

So, I called the people at the Scripps Cancer Center, and she "got" nine more years.

She was able to accomplish what she wanted thanks to research and stuff. She really put her heart into it and made the most of it. She got her wish, and she's my hero.

Ambassador of
Strength & Spirit

The Iron Woman Dominates ⟩ Dalani Kauihou Tanahy

AFTER WE FORMED the Westside Wahine Surf Club, we decided we wanted to have this all-women's surf meet. It was before women's surfing became so much in vogue and mainstream. It still kind of hadn't caught on.

We had to battle it out with all the Mākaha beachboys to have the contest. Getting a permit

from the city government was one thing, but getting permission from the beachboys was tough. We had to cry and beg to get them to let us have it.

Rell was through with the experimental cancer treatments in Houston, and, even though she was delighted to be home, the treatment had really taken it out of her. But, she was still smiling, even though her face was all swollen from the steroids she had to take in Houston. She was never *not* smiling, no matter what.

The night we were finishing setting up for the contest, putting up the big, colorful flags on bamboo poles and beautiful material to make it special, Rell showed up, smiling, saying, "I want to see how the waves are going to be for the contest."

So we said, "What? Are you competing?"

Still smiling, she said, "I had them let me go early. I told them I have to go home to compete in the contest."

So we said, "You're an animal. Okay, you go get 'em."

We had so much fun planning this thing, coming up with all kinds of fun divisions like "*menehune*," "*auntie*," "*tita*." Then, there was a special Iron Woman Division for the competitor who enters and wins in all the events: boogie board, shortboard and longboard.

So, the contest day comes, and we look at the list, and who is entered in all the divisions? Rell, fresh from her radical cancer treatment in Houston. And, compromised as she was, Rell killed it in every event and won the title. And we thought, "Okay, you really are an iron woman."

Surfing through the Blue
Rell Sunn via Bruce Jenkins

I ALWAYS TELL people that surfing saved my life when I was in a coma in Texas. I was seeing a powder blue, and I was dreaming that I was trying to catch waves out at Waikīkī. The water was powder blue and lots of sand under it, so it couldn't have been Mākaha, unless it was Point surf. I was just paddling and paddling. I could never catch a wave...just getting more and more frustrated.

It seemed like just a session, but, actually, my sister Val had been there a couple of days, and I'd been in this intensive-care unit.

Finally, one swell bumped up where it didn't really crest, but it caught me...and I stood up...and I was surfing.

I woke up, and I said, "Val, did you see that? I finally caught a wave!"

She was just beside herself. "Oh, Rell. We've been here for days. We thought you were gonna die."

I've always said surfing saved my life. It even kept me occupied while I was in a coma.

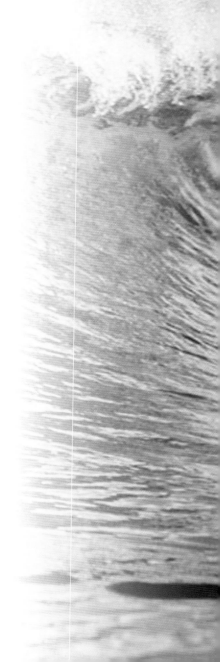

The Gift of a Comfortable Voice ⟩ Dennis Pang

MY DAD WAS going through prostate cancer for a whole year. Our family was on hold because everybody had to rally around…my mom…my family. Dad had just come out of the hospital, and we didn't know how to talk to him.

So, I called Rell to find out how to talk to him without feeling uncomfortable.

She coached me into relaxing and talking about my life and asking him how he's feeling— not to be intimidated talking about his problem. Just talk story; don't freak out; just relax.

She was diagnosed with cancer at that time, and she felt the vibe about everyone feeling uncomfortable talking to her. It's a common thing. People don't know what to say to their close friend. A lot just run away from talking with them because they don't know how to act.

I was kind of leaning toward that…intimidated because she was going through it herself. She was the victim of the problem…people coming up and talking to her and they weren't being themselves because they were uncomfortable.

She taught me to be cool with my dad. He passed away within a year after he was diagnosed. But, Rell gave me the gift of how to talk to him before he died.

A lot of people won't talk about the cancer, but she said, "I welcome people to talk about it and ask how I'm feeling." They wanted to talk to her because they loved her and they were her friends.

A Good Reason to Live 〈 Donald Takayama

WHEN RELL HAD this cancer and stuff, I'd call her up and go, "How you doing, Rell?"

She'd say, "I don't know. I'm not feeling too good."

So I'd go, "Rell, I'm making you one board you know."

And she'd go, "Nah, really?" She'd call me back later and say, "Hey, when my board going get *pau*?"

So, I'd say, "How you feeling?"

"Oh, bettah, bettah."

So, I shipped a board over to her.

"Wow. I'm going try 'em now."

"Let me know how it works."

Later, she'd go, "T'anks, I had so much fun."

But that's what it is—just keeping the heart and the mind going…the stoke. When someone is depressed, all is lost. So, I'd make these boards, and she'd get all excited. You've only got one life to live, and you've got to share it with everyone. And she was always sharing, always smiling.

Aloha ʻOe to the Queen of Mākaha 〉 Greg Ambrose

RELL SUNN'S LIFE ended in the same fashion she had lived it—on her terms. Sunn displayed a great many talents during her short life—radio surf reporter, disc jockey, TV commentator, star of videos and commercials, writer, Hōkūleʻa crew member, outrigger canoe paddler, hula dancer, international professional surfer, lifeguard, and schoolteacher. But, mostly, she was a Mākaha girl who saw the world yet never wanted to live anywhere but within bicycling distance of the surf at Mākaha.

The four Sunn sisters and their brother Eric grew up frolicking near their home in the waves at Mākaha Beach with the Keaulana clan. Although her mother and sisters moved to the neighbor islands to seek the old Hawaiʻi, Rell always found it at Mākaha.

Moku and Wally Froiseth's children also grew up surfing with Rell. That she would go on to become an international ambassador of *aloha* came as no surprise. "Even as a child, she was special," Moku said.

Teene Froiseth remembers when Rell became one of the city's first *wahine* lifeguards in 1977, the same year he started. "It was great to have Rell. Women have a way of settling down all the guys. Without her and without Pua Mokuau, it is distinctly different here at work. It's more of a boys' club. I liked it when she was out in the water. She always had the '*aloha* spirit.'"

Teene's sister Luana knew that Rell was always a home-girl at heart. "She traveled here and there and loved a lot of places, but nothing could beat surfing at Mākaha. She lived for surfing at Mākaha every day. Now, Mākaha is going to be a hard place to go out to because, for those of us who don't live out here, seeing Rella and talking story with Rella was something we all looked forward to."

Everyone was welcome at her Mākaha home, dubbed "Rell's Motel" because the world's most famous surfers, along with others who needed sanctuary from life's storms, found comfort and *aloha* there.

Rell helped save lives as a lifeguard, yet her greater talent was to change lives through her gentle yet magnetic personality. Her famed Menehune surf contests began as a birthday celebration for her young daughter, Jan, and grew to become a valuable lesson for thousands of Hawai'i's youngsters. They learned through friendly competition that everyone is a winner if they surf for the pure joy of it.

Rell worked hard to get enough *kokua* to take local *keiki* surfers to France for the Biarritz Surf Festival in 1995. She wanted to expand their cultural horizons and show the French wave riders how to surf with *aloha*. "The true spirit of surfing is in these kids," Rell said.

Rell had been his mentor through countless Menehune Contests since he was a toddler. "She was the ultimate to be around," Suratt said. "It made it special to have her there with us in France. She opened horizons for us, and those experiences helped me a lot."

Rell delivered her greatest gift after she was diagnosed with breast cancer at age thirty-three. While her life became a series of painful operations and treatments to stave off the dreadful disease, she used her ability to make people believe in themselves and in the healing power of love. When Rell asked Momi Keaulana, "Why has this happened to me?" Momi gently responded, "God has a plan for you."

Many of the older women on the Leeward side feel that, if you talk about something, you give it power over you. So, they keep quiet about their cancer, which makes it worse. Rell became a navigator with the Waiʻanae Cancer Research Center, visiting groups of women—aunties, cousins, and church gatherings—and telling them about cancer screening, detection, and treatment in a way that would make local people feel comfortable.

"I remember the day she called to tell me she had breast cancer," said Waiʻanae nurse practitioner Kathy Terada. "I thought, 'You can't, you are too young.' It was terrible how it happened, all the barriers and resistance she met. So, she told women those stories and talked about how we need to ask questions…we need to be responsible for our care." Terada's voice dropped to a barely audible whisper. "Pua and Rell were godmothers to my two boys and two of my best friends. I have learned so much from this and learned so much from them. The last time I saw Rell awake, she was still the most gracious person…to the very end."

Rell's middle name is Kapoliokaʻehukai, which means "heart of the sea." She drew strength from the ocean and passed that strength on to others. "How many lives were touched or saved or extended by her cancer education awareness work?" asked San Francisco oncologist Dr. Mark Renneker, who Rell's husband Dave Parmenter credits with being the person whose medical expertise and guidance did the most to prolong Rell's life.

"The cancer never conquered her spirit," said Parmenter. "She was indomitable. When the demons of fear came to her, she picked up the phone and called someone else and made them laugh and brightened their day."

As a nonsurfer, Tara Lee Torburn was at first unaware of Rell's status as a legendary surfer—one of the founders of the women's professional surfing circuit, a top competitor and prime practitioner of Hawaiian soul surfing, a tasteful, casual blend of performance, style, and grace under pressure. Torburn found all that out in 1989, when her Oceanside Longboard Surfing Club dedicated its annual contest to raising funds to pay for Rell's bone marrow aspiration in Texas. "It was the most incredible event I have ever been associated with," Torburn said. "I received donations and notes from people that poured forth from all over the world."

Eventually, the years of treatment took their toll and kept Rell from her beloved ocean. Two weeks before Thanksgiving, Luana Froiseth and a few friends took Rell for a last surf session at Mākaha. "Dave pushed her on the waves, and we paddled her back out. It was good fun," Luana said. As her condition worsened, Dave and Jan, who had protected Rell from well-wishers who might have unwittingly worsened her condition, began to let friends and family gather to share a special moment, in person when possible, by phone when necessary.

"There are good deaths and bad deaths, and this was a magnificent death," said Renneker, her oncologist. They carried her to the beach on New Year's Day to let her bask in the light of the sun setting over the ocean at Mākaha one last time.

"When you watch somebody so lively and vibrant suffer, that is the worst," said Momi Keaulana. "I asked Rella to do me a favor. I told her, 'You fought such a beautiful fight for so may years, but, when you are through, just close your eyes and go to sleep.' And that is what she did."

Early one Friday morning, Rell died. She was 47.

Tears from a Stone 〉 Jim Kempton

AT RELL'S FUNERAL SERVICE, everyone was starting to cry, and I was standing right next to Barry Kanaiaupuni, this gigantic, steely, Hawaiian dude, who I had always imagined as being friendly but just like a rock.

He's standing there and his cheek starts twitching, and, all of a sudden, he reaches into his pocket and puts his dark glasses on. He didn't want anybody to see him, but the tears were rolling right out. That was the kind of thing Rell could do to people.

Saving Lives ⟩ Judy Seladis-Cocquio

I DIDN'T KNOW who Rell was. I had not grown up in this area. My father was in the military, so we were living all over the place in Europe and the United States. I was just out of college, and, like anywhere else, people knew what I did, what my goals were. So, they just asked me if I would be interested in working as a researcher for breast cancer. I thought, "Oh, my gosh, okay." I interviewed for the position, and they told me I was hired…that I was the best candidate for the position. I met Rell through the project.

The first time that I went out on this research project, I was new to the community. I was given the job title of "documentator." I didn't now what a "documentator" was. But, they just said, "Let's evolve with it."

The first time I went out with Rell was to a senior citizens' group at this gymnasium in the Wai'anae area. Rell did some exercises with these senior citizens so they knew who she was. She said, "You know what? I want to talk about something that is really serious, and, just because you are seniors, that doesn't mean this doesn't happen to you. I'm going to talk about cancer."

We went that first day, and I said, "What do you want me to do, Rell?"

She said, "I don't know. Take their stories down, observe, whatever you want to do."

She gathered them in their chairs in a circle, and I kind of set myself outside of the group because I was just going to take notes. And, one of the seniors was very disturbed by that. They asked, "What is she doing sitting outside of the group? Is she with you or what?" So, Rell explained that I am part of the research project, and I was going to write down the stories. So, then, they wanted to know more about me. I told them I lived in the community, and I was currently working with the project that Rell is interested in.

They said, "No, no, no, we can't have you sitting outside the circle. You have to sit inside the circle with us." Then, Rell started navigating through this whole process of giving information and getting comments and stories.

She had a real talent for doing that. It wasn't like, "I know all the answers, and I'm going to give them to you." I just, very quietly, took down a lot of their stories and a lot of observations.

It lasted an hour. They couldn't take a lot of sitting for long. The *kokua* group brought food. That was very important as part of the group, part of the whole process. Not just any kind of food, it was taro, steamed taro, not a lot of the fatty stuff.

After that, we went back to the office for a debriefing session. It was really interesting how my role evolved by a comment from one of the seniors before we left. She said to me, "You know, you are the keeper of our stories, and you need to be very reverent about how you collect our stories because it's part of our lives, part of our spirit, part of our energy. So, be really reverent when you do a *kokua* group that you know that is your role and that it's important."

After that, we moved to a larger group with the other staff. There were three navigators, the people who would be doing the educational part of the project…going out to these women and touching base and giving out information. A lot of times, I would go with Rell because she asked me to be there. Because she felt very supportive, you wouldn't think she would get butterflies when she did her *kokua* group. But she did. She was uncertain about how to begin, about what the reaction of women might be.

I remember one evening we were doing a *kokua* group, and she said, if she saved even one woman, all the pain and suffering was worth it. That, to me, was very touching, knowing that she was going through her own personal struggle with cancer. A lot of the women who knew evidently knew her better than I did. They knew what she did and really respected her. But, they also were afraid of her. Like any other disease or illness, people think it's contagious. So, many were really afraid. Rell had to say, "This is not something you can catch. It's genetic; it's environmental. You cannot catch it from me. It's not like measles."

It was very hard for women to talk about their mothers, grandmothers, or aunts who died and no one ever knew why. They came to find out that many of the women died because they had breast cancer or cervical cancer. Hawaiian women seem to be high risk for those areas. Rell tried to get all the people she knew to do a *kokua* group so they could spread the information and put their fears aside. "Yeah, breast cancer is really scary. But, you catch it early enough, you can survive."

The project was created because, statistically, Hawaiian women were dying of breast cancer and cervical cancer, and a lot of them were not coming in to get checked. They wanted to find out what were the reasons for that. A lot of the reasons were religious. Their religious learning was primarily, "It's bad to touch yourself." So, you're asking these women to do a breast self exam, and they already know that means touching your body, and they're already thinking, "Hey, that's bad. That's not good."

Another obstacle was that you don't want to say the C-word, because that's like asking the disease to come into your family. A lot of them also were turned off by the way they were treated when they came in to the medical center. They weren't treated with respect; they were talked down to.

So, the project did it in an informal way, first by giving information. And a lot of them did not have health insurance. "How are you going to do this if you don't have health insurance? They don't have money to pay for that. Going to the doctor is a hardship unless you really, really need it. Money is to bring food to the table and clothe my kids." So, what we did was remove those obstacles, give them information, give them a voucher so they didn't have to pay for the exam, and, if they were found to have an abnormal pap smear or mammogram, then one of the navigators would go with them to the doctor as a support person.

Also, what the group did was help women to ask questions. Because the older generation, that includes my mom, felt like the doctor knows what he's doing, they thought, "I don't need to ask any questions." Yes, you do need to ask questions, and, if they don't have the answers, go to another doctor. Basically, what we did was literally take them one woman at a time through the health center to get a mammogram and a pap smear. Some of them hadn't been to the doctor in thirty years.

So, our project was being a support system, talking story, knowing there are people out in the community who can give you answers, helping you through the system, and being there for you. [This approach] really changed a lot in the way that doctors looked at their patients at the health center. It was an eye-opener for the physicians to look at what they were doing. A lot of the women felt uncomfortable with a male physician doing a pap smear or a mammogram.

They didn't know they could ask for a woman to do this. They didn't know how to ask for a female physician or nurse practitioner.

The project actually was not only an eye-opener to the health center but also to the people who participated in the project and the community. All of us realized that, in the medical system or the school system, people want to be respected. It doesn't matter what their income is or where they live, they should be treated with respect.

I think that, with Rell being out there and with her history, she had a big impact on the community with the project itself and on people. People looked at her as a seed of hope because she was still surviving after all this time. When people ask, "Are you still fighting your cancer?" she would say, "That's not an important question. The important thing is I'm here now."

One thing really stands out in my mind. After one treatment, I remember seeing her at the beach, and she was out catching a wave. I didn't think it was her. I happened to be at Mākaha Beach, and I was watching this woman surf. Then, she came in, and I said, "Oh, geez, Rell, I didn't realize it was you."

She had lost her long beautiful hair, but she didn't care. She sat down and said, "You know what, Judy? I think the battle is going to be over really soon. When you look out on the sunset and you're on the beach, remember me."

I remember her catching that wave. "That's all that matters—that I can still go out and catch a wave. When I have to go…." (She never said "die.") "When I have to leave, I want to see that last sunset."

I wanted to hug her and say, "You know what, Rell? I understand." But there weren't any words between us, just a look.

Before I knew that she died, one of her friends who did a *kokua* group found out she had cancer. But, it had advanced, and she had passed away before Rell did. Rell was devastated by it. She said, "You know, Judy, I had this dream. I saw Pua on the beach, and she was carrying her surfboard, and she was beckoning to me, and I said, 'No, I'm looking for a wave.' But, she's beckoning to me. What do you think that is all about?"

And, I knew, I thought that she was calling her, but I didn't tell her that. I said, "Well, I don't know. Maybe because you were so close to her and you miss her a lot." I think she knew that her time was getting closer. The last time she went in for an exam they said they found tumors in her throat, and it was going to be very hard for her to talk, and they wanted to do treatment, and there was a lot of risk involved, and she said, "Just as long as I can surf I'll be okay"

She always said, "We're twins, Judy."

And I said, "In what way, Rell?"

"Because we have the same birthday." I was older than her by a few years, but she told me, "Every time you celebrate your birthday, think of me." And I do. I always do. Rell was a sign of hope and strength and struggle. I know two more people who have cancer, and, when they talk about their own struggles, they say they feel close to Rell and they feel her strength.

Wouldn't Want to Miss a Minute ⟩ Linny Morris

WE DIDN'T HAVE the typical things in common. I didn't dance hula with her; I didn't surf; I didn't free dive. I didn't do any of that stuff, which was what all of her community saw in her—just her good-heartedness. I just saw this incredible, manic energy. For instance, Rell said Brian and Noble Keaulana's yard used to be a well-known eyesore on the street. "While they were away one day, I just couldn't stand it. So, I took my tools over there and cleaned their yard because I just couldn't bear looking at it one more minute," Rell said.

To me, that was the "Japanese *mama san*" side of her. Not that she was a Japanese *mama san*, but really wiry and spry and looking great into old age…in great shape and doing *tai chi* when you're eighty. She was that kind of person.

Somehow, I always thought she was going to make it. I was just so in denial. "No, this can't be happening." She was the one who was supposed to make it; there was supposed to be a miracle. She pulled it off a couple of times, and I'm sure it had to do with the fact that she was willing to do these really radical treatments. The contrast between her and Pua was so great. I can totally understand Pua's approach. Maybe Pua had a sense of feeling at peace—she already did what she needed to do in this lifetime, and she was ready to try the next thing. You know, that Hawaiian saying about changing address… perhaps Pua was ready to "change address" while Rell was fighting tooth and nail to stay here. She loved everything about life and didn't want to miss a minute of it.

The Goddess Becomes a Friend ⟩ Ron Mizutani

I THINK I WAS like many other thousands of local boys who had an amazing crush on this local goddess. When we were growing up, Rell Sunn was every local boy's dream girl—surfer girl, beautiful *wahine*.

Later, in my professional life, I got the call one day that Rell was going to be my co-host for this canoe race. I was so exited about the opportunity to work with her. My first true meeting with her was on Moloka'i. And there we were. We all met at the Kalua Koi hotel at the old Sheraton.

She walked up to me and said, "*Aloha*, Ron, I'm Rell."

And I said, "Yeah, I know." I was in awe.

There was a three to five foot swell going on right outside the hotel, and we were both looking at the waves. Then, she looked at me and said, "You wanna go surf?"

I said, "But, I don't have a board."

"No worry," she said.

Then, she walked down to the beach, and, in a matter of seconds, people were saying, "Auntie Rell, you wanna use my board?" In twenty minutes, we were out in the lineup. I'll never forget that moment sitting in the lineup with her. I couldn't believe I was surfing with the queen of

Mākaha, let alone knowing that, tomorrow morning, we were going to be out in the *Ka Iwi* together as co-hosts of the show.

In that hour and a half in the lineup, she gave me so many waves—the sets and everything. Everybody was pulling back when they saw it was her. And she would say, "Go Ronnie! Go Ronnie!" blocking it off for me.

I was going, "Oh, my gosh. I can't believe I'm surfing with her." That day was very special for me. We just talked about our lives and our careers. I had known already that she was diagnosed with cancer, and I was just amazed by this woman who you wouldn't even know had cancer. Only later did I find out that she was already suffering. She was coping with cancer and not just living with it.

As the years went by, we did several *Na Wahine o ke Kai*'s together, and it was during those many hours on the ocean that she would share so much about her knowledge of the ocean and currents and how to read the wind. I had not begun paddling. I had paddled, but not at that intense level of competition. It was Rell who convinced me on one of those days to try it—to do *Moloka'i*. I'll never forget her words: "No regrets, Ronnie. Don't have any regrets." I always told her, later on, before she passed, that she was the one who inspired me to do the *Ka Iwi*, the *Moloka'i Ho'e* for the men's race, and, that's when I handed in my microphone and grabbed a paddle instead. It was 1997 that I did my first *Moloka'i*. It was through Rell's inspiration and words and encouragement.

One *Na Wahine*, there was real speculation whether she was going to join us. She was not well.

So, I called her and said, "You know what? You don't have to come."

She said, "No, I need to be there."

This was like her own "beach break." We used to do a segment on KHON called "Beach Break," and, when things got too stressful, she would say, "I need my 'beach break.'" The ocean was keeping her alive…and all her missions and touching lives in the meantime. I was told she was vomiting. So, it was up in the air whether she was going to come.

On Friday, they said she was coming. So, we went up to Moloka'i. She was really self-conscious about her looks because she had no hair that trip, and I said, "Ah, you look beautiful." That was the trip that just blew me away.

Here we are on the *Ka Iwi*. She's suffering; my cameraman gets seasick off *Hale o Lono* Harbor; and she's caring for my cameraman for the next seven hours. He's puking his brains out, and Rell's out there every twenty minutes running to him, making sure he's hydrated. I'm going, "What's wrong with this picture?" This woman is dying, and my cameraman is getting cared for.

That is how much *aloha* this lady had, not to mention the words she chose every time we did a segment. We were constantly doing updates throughout the race. And, not only does she know the ocean, but she also knows everybody in the ocean. Talk about a professional. It was obvious she did her homework, and I admired that a lot. She'd come to the table every show, no matter what show.

She knew everybody in the canoe seats. "Okay, seat five is so and so. She just gave birth three weeks ago, and she's hammering out here."

I'm like, "How do you know that?"

It was totally amazing how much of a professional she was…and just as real.

That show she closed off, and she said something I used in her obituary later on. It was like *chicken skin*. I sat there dumbfounded when she said it.

"No matter where we are, no matter what we're doing, no matter who we're with, when the wind is blowing you'll always think of the *Ka Iwi*."

I was like, "Wow. Was she saying goodbye to me just now, and goodbye to all of us?"

She looked at me and said, "Ronnie, it was truly a pleasure."

I started bawling. I couldn't talk. I didn't know what to say. So, we had to re-cut the footage. We did a little edit there because I was just so floored.

We held a long embrace, and we cried, and then…I'm gonna start crying…but this is the amazing thing. I was just, "Oh, my god. This lady is amazing. She just gave eight hours of her time on the ocean back to the women to share her last show because she knew how important it was for her to be there." And I didn't understand how special that day was for me until she passed.

When she did pass away, I got the call. Dave asked me if I would read the eulogy. He wrote the words, and I just tried to deliver it. I was so touched. I said, "Dave, there are tons of people out there who were closer to Rell than I was."

But, he said, "No, you were very special to her. And, these words, I know you will deliver them from the heart."

I've done a few eulogies through the years, and I've never felt so honored to share such powerful words. He wrote an incredible eulogy. That day, when we said goodbye to Rell, there were so many tears on the beach and so many stories being shared. I remember our canoe broadcasting crew was there, everyone who had worked through the years with Rell. Talk about a big *pā'ina*. It was full of happiness for her life and celebrating her life, but, at the same time, we knew we had lost a very special lady in our lives.

It was only then that I really, truly realized how much of an impact she had on me. Now, there isn't a day that, when I go to *Ka Iwi*, and I've done about ten channels now since, that I don't say a prayer for her. When I jump in that ocean during an ocean change, my first change is for Rella. I always get in that boat and I thank her—I thank *akua*, and I thank Rell, in that order, for inspiring me to be in the ocean and competing at a top level. It was the women, it was *nā wāhine o ke kai* that inspired this guy, and it was the queen of Mākaha who inspired me to perpetuate my culture as much as I could. I cannot talk about her and not cry because the woman who I had a crush on growing up…who I fell in love with…was a dear friend.

Hana Hou ⟩ Tara Torburn

THE LAST TIME I saw Rell in the hospital was when I flew over the coloring books we used to do for Rell's Menehune Contest, the ones with the 'ukulele songs. It was just after Rell was off being interviewed for that documentary by Charlotte Lagarde. Every day, she used to call and tell me, "I am so tired. I wish these girls would finish this. I am so tired."

Finally, they finished. Rell goes into the hospital, and I'm supposed to come over to help with the Menehune Contest. I had to bring the coloring books to assemble them there because I had them printed on the mainland so I hadn't had time to assemble them yet. Claudia Woo and Keith picked me up at the airport. I was staying with them, so we stuck all these books together.

I told the Westside Wahines, "If you want me to stay and help with the contest, I'll stay. Otherwise, I'm leaving because Dave can't handle me being around here."

And they said, "No, we've done this enough. We know what we're doing."

I wanted to see Rell. She was in intensive care, and Dave said, "You can't go. No one is allowed in except family."

I said, "Look, I'm going to go. Claudia and Keith said they'll take me. If I can't go in, fine. But, I promised Rell I'd see her on this trip."

So, we go up to the intensive-care unit, and there is no one around. I get off the elevator, and I hear, "Where's Tara? She promised she was going to come."

I look at Claudia and Keith, and I go, "And Dave said I wasn't supposed to see her."

I walk in, and her mom's there, and Jan's there. I brought her a *tiki*, and her mom flipped out because she never liked her *tikis*. The year before, [Rell] had given me some money to buy a Hawaiian heirloom bracelet, and she let me put her middle name on it. So, I was showing that to her, and I showed her the *'ukulele* coloring book and a bunch of other things. When she finally did go home and wasn't on the morphine drip anymore, she said, "Tara, it was like psychedelic. You showed me all this stuff, and I was seeing all these colors."

I had a long talk with Momi Keaulana the day before Rell's service, and we both agreed that, even though Dave kept a lot of people away from Rell, his main goal was keeping her alive, and I think he kept her alive as long as possible.

Too Busy Living ⟩ Tara Torburn

WHEN RELL WAS going through her radiation treatment, we would always seem to be on the North Shore at Hale'iwa surfing. She'd come in and go, "Oh no! We need to be in town [for a doctor's appointment]." So, we'd jam over, run in the back hallways of Queens hospital, and run into the room. She would always be late for her appointments, which messed everyone else up.

There was a two-week period where we were going every day for treatment. You always had your appointment at the same time, and the same two women were always there. I saw these two women getting sicker and sicker. They would just look at her. Rell comes running in, and, of course, they knew Rell's story. This was not her first time here; she's had these bone marrow transplants and this and that.

Rell would run into the dressing room and drop everything, while I'd go to the waiting room. The women would look at me and say, "How does she do it?"

I'd say, "If I knew, I'd put it in a bottle and give it away to everyone."

But, no matter how much of a hurry she was in, Rell always took time to talk with people. One day, a woman saw her and said, "You're Rell Sunn. Can I talk to you for a minute?"

So, she sat down and spent time with this woman. She always had the perfect thing to say.

Rell's Next Trip Around
Sonja Evensen & Marilyn Link

MARILYN: The last time I saw Rell, I think there was a clue she knew she wasn't coming back from her cancer. She said to me, "Look at my feet," and she had those veins on her feet. She said, "When you get these, it means you're going to die."

I said, "Oh, Rell, it doesn't mean that."

Why would I say that? What I should have done was thrown her over my shoulder and walked her down to the beach and said, "Okay, you're gonna die? Here's the ocean."

SONJA: One time she told me she was standing in line somewhere and some complete stranger came up and told her that she was a very old soul.

MARILYN: Oh, that was her hands. She had old hands and old feet. She told me once what it meant. When you have old hands and old feet it means you're an old soul. I don't think this was Rell's first trip.

SONJA: I miss Rell, but I still have Rell. I can still conjure her up. I can still have the sense of humor, the way she had of looking at things. I can recreate some of that. That's a gift that she leaves behind. So, that thing of you dying and that's it—there's some stuff that's still here.

MARILYN: And all the people that she connected are still here.

Dancing on Water ⟩ Warren Bolster

WE CAME ALL the way to China on a surf trip, and Rell didn't care that the waves weren't that good because she was so stoked to be in her grandmother's country. It was so important for her that she went that she stopped her cancer treatments. It meant the world to her.

The other surfers on the trip were bummed that the waves weren't good, but she couldn't have cared less. We were all in awe of her.

Beijing was difficult. They spoke a different dialect. But, we went to the Forbidden City, the zoo, saw the pandas, went to Tiananmen Square three years before the protests.

We, then, went to Guangzhou, the old Canton, which meant another new dialect. We had translators for translators. Then, we flew to Hainan, a third dialect. So, now we had translators for translators for translators. They were government G-men who were very low key, but machine guns were everywhere. It was unbelievable. Everywhere we drove, we drove in second gear.

There's a photo of her on the beach at Hainan. The titanium miners gathered on the beach and would not leave until she came back from surfing.

[The people there] were just fascinated by this girl, the Chinese officials and the photographers and the interpreters. They were struck by how romantically we talked about surfing. They interviewed us and asked why we talked so romantically about the sport.

Rell was like a goddess on the beach to the Chinese. It was unbelievable. Every picture you see with the Chinese around, they all looked at Rell. All they focused on was Rell. They didn't ignore the rest of us, but it was all about Rell…dancing on water.

Reminiscing About Mom ⟩ Jan Sunn

MY MOM HAS taught me many things. The lessons that she gave I will cherish always. From respect and generosity to love and laughter, from fight and cry to discipline and nurture, from responsibility and independence to humility and curiosity, from the adventures to come to the simplicity of life. The simple wonders of just flipping over a rock in the tide pools and seeing another world will stay with me forever. I remember the Easter egg hunts at these tide pools and just getting the community, the extended family and friends, together for some great, hysterical times. We'd do firecrackers on New Year's and the 4th. We'd have Halloween parties and tea parties. Then, we'd pick *limu kohu* and have *limu* card making parties. I loved picking flowers for hula, having emptying-the-net parties, and catching the first wave of the New Year.

She showed me how to find octopus in the ocean and how to spear a stickfish. (My favorite! It tasted just like chicken! Swear!) And she showed me how to clean our catch. (Not my favorite!) I learned how to make huge fish scale earrings from her big *uhu* catch, how to make a game out of raking the plumerias in the front yard, how to hang clothes in the back, how to deal with the cane spiders in the outside shower, how to spear a rat in the garage roof, and how to hunt for "specific" items at garage and estate sales. Most of all, she showed me how important it was to just sit and breathe during a sunset and sunrise. I could go on forever with the lessons I learned from my mom, lessons she made fun and special just for me.

Some stories that I will always remember and hold dear are the ones she would come home with after traveling. It would absolutely break my heart when she left. As I would wait, lots of thoughts would come to mind, "Why did she leave me?" "Why didn't she take me?" They were very confusing times for me, to say the least. But, all those questions got answered as I got older. As mad as I would be when she came home, she would always have the ultimate story of her adventure on that last trip. These stories would always make me think of a Japanese floating glass ball. As I got older, I realized that this glass ball was meant to be her—simple… fragile…yet strong…. This glass ball would float from sea to sea and surf the best waves and visit the most beautiful oceans in the world and, yet, would always come home to me…to Mākaha…to Hawaiʻi. It would come home a little different every time with a crack here, a chip there, a barnacle here. But, every time, it was her, basically unchanged only wiser. She pulled me into her stories as if I were there. Sometimes, I was actually fortunate enough to go on a surf trip with her, and it would be amazing.

Now, I can only hope that I've taken the best stories and knowledge from her and passed them on to my *keiki* so that they will always have a little piece of their *kupuna* in their hearts. I see so much of her in them that it makes me glow.

THE FOLLOWING INDIVIDUALS are credited for graciously contributing photographs, professionally shot and candidly captured, of the amazing Rell Sunn.

Bernie Baker
Ron Brazil
Warren Bolster
Burl Burlingame
Jeannie Chesser
Mark Cunningham
Jeff Divine
Sonja Evensen
Ralph Goto
Ken Ige
Tom Keck
John Moore
Linny Morris
Puggy Pugadillio
Judy Seladis-Cocquio
Kathy Terada
Tara Torburn
Dan Fletcher - Painting - "Rell Rides the Skies"
Caroline Zimmerman - Painting - "Little Hula Heaven"